Praise for
A Dangerous Faith

"A riveting real-life read. If you love adventure and great stories, you'll find this a very instructive and encouraging book."

—Dr. Dennis Rainey, president, FamilyLife

"Peb Jackson, being a lifelong adventurer himself, is probably the best person alive to have written *A Dangerous Faith*. He's a dangerous guy who has lived God's call to a manly and spiritual faith—a life of risk and full throttle commitment."

—Bob Buford, founder of Leadership Network
and author of *Halftime* and *Finishing Well*

"These gripping stories of adventure are more than just fluff. Each one is infused with powerful faith principles that will make every man see his life in a different light. Whether you are a pencil pusher or Indiana Jones, you'll be challenged by this book!"

—Chuck Holton, author, CBN correspondent,
and former U.S. Army Airborne Ranger

"As a big fan of survival stories, such as *Into Thin Air* and *The Perfect Storm*, I was thrilled to discover this riveting collection. These true-life accounts deal with man versus nature, man versus himself, and ultimately man in his quest to know God. With writing that hammers and sparkles, *A Dangerous Faith* is a must for any man's collection."

—Eric Wilson, author of *A Shred of Truth*
and *Facing the Giants*

"*A Dangerous Faith* is a gripping tapestry of stories weaving the power of prayer and true life experiences. These stories will motivate and encourage you to be prayer heroes in dealing with your own personal risks in order to do extraordinary things and see God's reward."

—JOHN LIND, president/CEO, The Presidential Prayer Team

"Too often we think of Christianity as safe, the stuff of felt boards and high teas. How refreshing to see Christians living on the edge, where life can be extinguished in an instant and where the answers aren't so simple. Come meet the robust Savior we serve, the originator and giver of a dangerous faith."

—JEFFERSON SCOTT, author of the Operation: Firebrand series

"It was inspiring to see these examples of God's power sustaining through crises and changing people in unexpected ways."

—C. SCOTT HARRISON, MD, president, CURE International

"*A Dangerous Faith* is a wonderful read that will captivate the hearts and minds of the reader. The stories revel at the intersection of human courage and divine intervention. This is a wonderful read for all!"

—RICHARD SAVIDGE, vice president, Generous Giving

A DANGEROUS
FAITH

A DANGEROUS FAITH

TRUE STORIES OF ANSWERING THE CALL TO ADVENTURE

JAMES LUND & PEB JACKSON

WATERBROOK
PRESS

A DANGEROUS FAITH
PUBLISHED BY WATERBROOK PRESS
12265 Oracle Boulevard, Suite 200
Colorado Springs, Colorado 80921
A division of Random House Inc.

In a few cases, names have been changed to protect the identities of the persons involved.

ISBN-13: 978-0-7394-9546-9

Note: Failure to apply the principles of risky faith contained herein could result in a seriously underdeveloped spiritual life. Any resemblance to actual biblical principles is entirely intentional.

Printed in the United States of America

To all the souls who long for adventure and have—only temporarily—misplaced their courage and faith.

Jim: To my wife, Angela, who took the greatest risk of all in marrying me.

Peb: To my dad, Dr. Sheldon Jackson. You set the example for me in your pursuit of knowledge, love of life, audacious commitment to my mother, and contagious demonstration of God's love to the very end.

CONTENTS

ACKNOWLEDGMENTS

Jim Lund: Little did I know eight years ago, when I first started thinking about the relationship between risk and faith, where God would lead me. My thoughts, supercharged by a reading of Jon Krakauer's *Into Thin Air*, began moving in the direction of a book. That led to a conversation with Doug Gabbert, then an executive at Multnomah Books and one of my bosses. Doug introduced me to an amazing adventurer named Peb Jackson, who put me in touch with another incredible trailblazer named Gil McCormick, and our expedition in pursuit of a book was off.

The trail has taken more twists and turns than a roller coaster, and we would never have made it without the help of many guides. In particular, thanks go to:

- Doug Gabbert, for introducing me to a new partner and friend.
- Each of the courageous men and women featured in this book, especially Gil and Leona McCormick, Steve Van Meter, Jim Nowak, Dave Anderson, Chris Braman, Sheila Moody, Bruce Olson, Ted Roberts, Carrie McDonnall, Matt Moseley, Boyd Clines, Brian Shul, and Bruce and Sheila Hendricks.
- My reading team: Dave Lund, Angela Lund, Bert Lund, Betty Lund, Erik Lund, David Schlatter, Tom Showalter, Paulmer Soderberg, Bob Green, Jeff Hiersche, Jeff Gerke, Stan Dean, and my "climbing" buddies, Larry Libby and Brian Thomasson.
- Bill Jensen, our agent and so much more: mentor, visionary, encourager, critic, fishing guide, friend. Bill, you da man!
- My wife, Angela, who supported me even when it looked like trying to write this book was a foolish dream, and my children whom I'm so proud of, Erik, Sonja, and Peter, who had to wait on too many evenings for Dad to get home.
- My parents, Bert and Betty Lund, who passed on their love of books

and learning to their son. Year after year, you both set the example
I try to live up to—thank you!

- Dave Kopp, for wise counsel and free lunches.

- Our fine editor at WaterBrook, Mick Silva, who caught the vision for
this project from the beginning and skillfully guided it all the way
home. Hey, Mick, we finally got to do a book together!

- Everyone on the great team at WaterBrook who had a hand in making this possible, including Joel Kneedler, Steve Reed, Leah McMahan,
Pam Shoup, and Karen Sherry.

- Jodi Carroll, who kept her sense of humor through my countless
phone calls and requests and always found a way to track down the
elusive Mr. Jackson. Thanks, Jodi!

- Peb Jackson, a guy who lives a dangerous faith every day and has
inspired me in so many ways. Peb, it's been a pleasure. I hope we
get to do it again soon.

Last, and most certainly not least, thanks to the Lord, who pushed me to
keep going when I was ready to give up. This is for Him.

Peb Jackson: My father was a college professor who had a PhD in history and
loved books. At least once a year, he removed his "professorial robes" (so to
speak) and took my twin brother, Shel, and me on adventures. (My mother
and younger sister, Marilyn, usually engaged in less risky pursuits.) It might've
been fishing for salmon off the coast of Oregon or crossing a raging river on a
log. I suspect there were other outings he involved me in as a small child that
are not part of my present memory, but nevertheless instilled a thirst for risk
and adventure. Thanks, Dad.

During the next stage of my adventuring, Dr. Orv Mestad traveled with
me and other friends to Patagonia and the east face of Mount Whitney, as well
as on flights in his airplane to the Wind River Range in Wyoming. Orv was
passionate about fly-fishing, cycling, and mountains. He was a mentor and
partner and remains a dear friend.

My pursuits became even more serious as I met others who seemed larger than life. Tim Hansel of Summit Expedition and John Patten of Adventurous Christians fired my imagination from simmer to white-hot regarding climbing and introduced me to a community of hard-core Christian climbers who probably had as much influence on me as any group ever has. From this sprang a relationship with Dick Savidge that included many climbing adventures and not a few misadventures. Hugo Schoellkopf and Tony Wauterlek helped introduce me to the world of fly-fishing and hunting. Hugo died in an airplane crash in 1987, but for me his legacy in these areas continues. Tony and I have traveled from England to Alaska to Patagonia. He was always ready to go with passport in hand. Dr. Scott Harrison introduced me to the world of big-game hunting in Africa that resulted in the Cape buffalo story in this book. Others who have accompanied me are Joe and Noah Ritchie, Foster and Steve Friess, Rick Christian, Kevin Cusack, and Rick Melson. All of these guys are devoted to experiencing the fullness of adventure, yet also compassionate in giving time and resources to less fortunate and less fearless followers of Christ.

There are dozens of cyclists, including my first gurus, Jim and Barb Carlson, and the irrepressible Tom Ritchey, who are part of a Moab, Utah, "Feast of the Heart" group. Gil McCormick, Carl Yarbrough, and John Dozier were among the leading suspects in "enabling" me to follow my cycling-adventure passions. Jim Bisenius has been a co-conspirator on many fly-fishing adventures from Alaska to Costa Rica to Christmas Island to the Seychelles. He is also emblematic of many of my friends, brothers who stick together through thick and thin. Denver Darling is a buddy I could count on to join me when I would call and say, "I've got a trip you cannot refuse."

For the last ten years, I have met almost every Monday morning with a group of men from my neighborhood, and together we launch into the adventure of exploring Scripture and its application to our daily lives. Thank you Jim Brooke, Drew Wills, Ed Poremba, Rick Risk, Dave Stieber, Mike McCann, Phil Lane, Scott Blackmun, Ken Beach, Dave Lynch, Mike Murphy, Jeff Jenks, Russ Acuff, Dennis Fitzgerald, and Fred Stoot.

For the past several summers, Bill George and a bunch of young turks including his son Jon have joined me in climbing fourteeners in Colorado.

The attraction is mountain climbing, but the real substance is diving deep into issues of life and faith during the journey.

Most recently, Jim Lund has been my co-laborer on this project, doing the lion's share of the work but sharing with me a passion for the theme.

Lastly, I thank my beautiful wife of thirty-seven years, Sharon, at times an adventurer's widow who amazingly—and perhaps sometimes improbably—encouraged my wanderlust. Thanks, honey.

INTRODUCTION

Peb Jackson: A fierce wind whipped against my pajamas, and the tornado siren wailed as I held my father's hand and raced across the yard for the cellar under the guesthouse. I was a small boy in the little town of Haviland, Kansas, encountering real danger for the first time. I remember cowering in the dark cellar, feeling both afraid and thrilled.

As a boy, I always seemed to find opportunities to rediscover that thrill. I'd run across a road when a big truck was coming. I'd walk along a railroad track while a train headed my way. I'd climb the outside ladder rungs of the ten-story water tower at the center of town. I also tried, several times, to hold a cherry-bomb firecracker for as long as I could. Once I held on too long; the explosion lacerated my fingers. Yet that was part of the allure. The danger was real, and so were the consequences.

One other example stands out to me. When I was thirteen, I was driving a tractor and pulling a plow on my uncle's farm. What could be more boring than trying to maintain a straight line in a field for twelve hours? Then I spotted a group of young rabbits darting in alarm from the noise. I somehow tied the steering wheel down and kept the tractor and plow moving while I jumped off, chased down a couple of the rabbits, and jumped back onto the tractor in front of the lethal plow, grinning in triumph. Again, the proximity to risk and its consequences was powerfully attractive.

My fascination with adventure and danger was further fed by reading Edgar Rice Burroughs's Tarzan books and Maurice Herzog's mountaineering classic *Annapurna*. When my father took my twin brother and me on backpacking trips around the Grand Tetons, I imagined myself climbing the heights in the Himalayas with Herzog and other explorers. It was the beginning of a lifelong dedication to pursuing and uncovering the benefits of risk.

Jim Lund: I wasn't as daring as Peb while growing up, but I do recall, as a boy, following a local lad into a hidden tunnel on an Oregon beach and discovering that it stretched far longer and deeper than I could have imagined. Like Peb, I shuddered with a wonderful mixture of fear and excitement. Who knew what lay ahead in that unexpected labyrinth beneath the sand?

Also like Peb, as a youth I was enraptured by tales of marvels and risk and daring: books about dinosaurs and the Hardy boys, TV shows like *Voyage to the Bottom of the Sea* and *Star Trek*. I wanted to be there with Frank and Joe, with captains Crane and Kirk, solving mysteries and exploring the farthest reaches of sea and space.

Many years later, my eight-year-old, Peter, and I were riding our "trail bikes"—a pair of beat-up Magnas—down a dusty path on U.S. forest land in central Oregon. We dodged the outstretched branches of juniper trees as we flew along and kept a wary eye out for a recently sighted cougar.

We crested a hill, and there, hidden in the trees on our left, was a huge formation of rocks that practically screamed out the words "Climb me!" In an instant, Peter had dropped his bike and was running for them. "C'mon, Dad!" he yelled. It was vintage Peter, a boy who's constantly veering off-trail to explore a cave, a bug, a shadow, a sound, or whatever else strikes his imagination.

Then came the moment I remember best from that afternoon. As he ran, Peter twisted his torso for a glance back at me. He didn't speak, but his look said it all: *Are you coming, Dad? I'm not quite sure what's ahead, but I can't wait to check it out—as long as you're with me.*

Isn't that a picture from some point in all our childhoods? We're curious, ready for adventure, excited about the possibilities, thrilled with the hunt. Suddenly, in the midst of the journey, a sliver of doubt needles in. *Hey, there might be danger here—do we know what we're getting into?* But a glance reassures. *There's Dad. It's okay. So let's go!*

We're all born with that sense of curiosity, with an instinctive need to stretch and learn and discover. It's one of God's gifts for this life. Sadly, most of us grow out of it. We become analytical, judgmental, protective. We fear what failure will do to us or make us look like to others, never mind that failure is one of our greatest teachers.

Worst of all, in that critical moment of doubt, we forget what we knew to do instinctively as children—to look for Dad. Then it meant making eye contact with our earthly father. Today it means seeking and connecting with our Father in heaven.

God created us with this innate desire to risk. It's what makes us grow, spiritually and otherwise. Taking risks for His sake brings Him glory. Remembering to "look for Dad" draws us closer to Him.

Peb: Sharon, my wife of thirty-seven years, has joined me on some of my adventures, though she never really gets excited about cold, pain, and fatigue the way I do. But she gave me one of the most important verses of my life, one I quote often to anyone who will listen:

> He who forms the mountains,
>> creates the wind,
>> and reveals his thoughts to man,
> he who turns dawn to darkness,
>> and treads the high places of the earth—
>> the LORD God Almighty is his name.
>
> (Amos 4:13)

God formed each of us and the wondrous world we inhabit. He also gave us a passion to learn and explore. It was no accident. It's our pathway to faith.

Jim: *Risk. Adventure. Danger.* We don't normally associate those words with a devout faith. But in reality, the explorer and the believer are both walking the same path. The life of faith *is* a daring adventure, full of risk and danger. Jesus said: "Risk your life and get more than you ever dreamed of. Play it safe and end up holding the bag" (Luke 19:26, MSG).

The disciples risked everything to follow Christ. So did Stephen, Paul, and the other believers of the early church. In the first century, Paul wrote: "Who shall separate us from the love of Christ? Shall trouble or hardship or persecution or famine or nakedness or danger or sword? As it is written: 'For your sake we face death all day long'" (Romans 8:35–36).

In the sixteenth century, Martin Luther wrote: "Faith is a living, daring confidence in God's grace, so sure and certain that the believer would stake his life on it a thousand times."

At the beginning of the twenty-first century, author John Eldredge wrote in *Wild at Heart*: "Adventure, with all its requisite danger and wildness, is a deeply spiritual longing written into the soul of man."

Today, our need to risk and to fulfill that adventurous, spiritual longing is just as great, and just as necessary. We're not all equipped with the skills or mind-set to climb Mount Everest, dive to the ocean depths, or hunt Cape buffalo, and that's okay. But too many of us aim to avoid risk entirely. We've worked hard to achieve what we already have—relationships, status, possessions. We don't want to put our comfortable lifestyles in jeopardy. Yet as we struggle to preserve our complacent existence, we miss out on the amazing rewards of risk. What rewards? Everything that matters—the fully developed faith, joy, and blessings God intends for each of us.

Faith in God is much more than sitting through a church service each Sunday. We are more than "pew potatoes." Our faith must be active: "Seek me and live" (Amos 5:4). We're not watching a TV show or attending a concert; we're participating in a great hunt. We are called to *pursue* a dangerous faith, living every thought, every activity, and every moment at risk for the Lord.

It may mean speaking up when you'd rather be quiet. Or quitting a job to preserve your integrity. Or revealing your deepest fear to your spouse. It is an intentional stretching of long-held beliefs. Only here, on the precipice between the comfortable and the unknown, will faith truly thrive. Only here will you discover the ironic truth: the more you risk and trust God, the closer you move to His heart—and the safer you become.

Peb: I probably have a couple hundred books on climbing and adventure, but few mention faith. It is a remarkable omission. Can you imagine the people fighting for their lives in *Into Thin Air*, Jon Krakauer's account of the 1996 tragedy on Everest, *not* reflecting on the afterlife and their relationship to God or not calling on God for help in those desperate circumstances? The more I thought about this, the more I felt the need for a book about men and women of faith who are attracted to dangerous pursuits. When I learned that Jim was on a similar trail, we joined forces.

The exploration of faith is, in fact, the greatest adventure of all. It means going all out, not just in our "spiritual" endeavors but in every aspect of life. It means allowing the challenge of adventure to hone us so that we are equipped each day to cope with life's obstacles and opportunities.

The following true stories feature men and women who understand what I'm saying. They have answered the call to explore, to discover, and to seek God in the hard places. They are living out a bold, risk-filled faith—and have found their lives forever changed by the experience. Not all of them expected to meet God on their adventures, yet they all uncovered a holy reward beyond what they'd imagined.

Each of their stories is followed by a few closing comments from Jim or me on the practical applications of a dangerous faith. There are no dull moral lessons here. Instead, we offer what we hope are tools for *your* journey. When you accept this dangerous calling, we believe you'll discover, as I did, that the unvarnished Christ becomes even more alluring. You will be drawn into a faith—and a life—so boldly, so completely, that a personal relationship with God becomes irresistible. You'll be risking everything for what really matters. May these words inspire you to leave the comfortable life behind and dive headlong into complete trust in Him.

One Good Shot

BY PEB JACKSON WITH JAMES LUND

The Cape buffalo of Africa is born mean and grows more ornery by the day. The adult male is black and massive, two thousand pounds of flesh and hair and bone. He stands five feet at the shoulder and stares at potential victims out of malevolent brown eyes. His two heavy horns, which curve down from each side of the buffalo's head, then up and in, may span a meter in length. They're effective for killing a lion—or a man. The buffalo doesn't really care which.

Many consider the Cape buffalo the most dangerous animal in the world to hunt. He's aggressive and stubborn. His hide is at least an inch thick; it's rare to take him in one shot. When wounded and enraged, he's likely to charge at the shooter. Sometimes he'll keep coming after ten shots. I read about one that didn't stop even after fourteen 500-grain bullets entered his body. The fifteenth finally got him.

They say Cape buffaloes have killed more hunters in Africa than any other animal. I heard about an American who was on safari in Tanzania the week after we hunted the same area. He was standing near the woods, minding his own business, when a Cape buffalo suddenly charged out of the trees, knocked him down, and gored him to death. No one knew what provoked the brute to attack. No one even had a chance to raise a rifle.

Robert Ruark, the author and hunter, wrote, "I don't know what there is about buffalo that frightens me so. Lions and leopards and rhinos excite me but don't frighten me. But that buff is so big and mean and ugly and hard to stop, and vindictive and cruel and surly and ornery. He looks like he hates you personally. He looks like you owe him money. He looks like he is hunting you."

I think about all this as I lie in my cabin on a cool evening in Zimbabwe. It's September 15, 2005. I'm on safari. I've traveled ten thousand miles by jet, prop plane, Land Rover, and my own two feet for the chance to face off against this mighty beast of the bush. Tomorrow, it's my turn.

I wonder if I'll sleep at all tonight.

My friend Denver Darling had his turn today. On foot, we stalked herds of buffalo for six hours without firing a single shot—the animals were restless and kept moving. One moved closer than we'd have liked. From the bush, an enormous bull elephant suddenly charged at us, bellowing in anger, his ears flayed back and tusks out. At the time, fortunately, we were in the Land Rover with the engine already running, enabling a hasty retreat. It was a roaring reminder that we were treading on someone else's turf.

As I lie on the cot, listening to the late-evening snorts of colobus monkeys and the cackles of hyenas, I recall the safari tales of Ruark and Teddy Roosevelt and every hunting story I've ever read. I feel a kinship with all of them. I linger on the memory of another Ruark passage:

> Deep in the guts of most men is buried the involuntary response to the hunter's horn, a prickle of the nape hairs, an acceleration of the pulse, an atavistic memory of his fathers, who killed first with stone, and then with club, and then with spear, and then with bow, and then with gun, and finally with formulae. How meek the man is of no importance; somewhere in the pigeon chest of the clerk is still the vestigial remnant of the hunter's heart; somewhere in his nostrils the half-forgotten smell of blood. There is no man with such impoverishment of imagination that at some time he has not wondered how he would handle himself if a lion broke loose from a zoo and he were forced to face him without the protection of bars or handy, climbable trees.

The minutes tick by as I consider what may happen in a few hours. I wonder if I'll have my chance to answer the hunter's horn. I wonder how I'll handle myself if I do.

I don't know, of course, lying there contemplating my stalk of the Cape buffalo, imagining the adventure of a lifetime, that another hunter is already stalking me.

After a restless night, I'm up before 5 a.m. The camp is situated on flat terrain near the banks of a hundred-foot-wide stream, deep in the Zimbabwe bush. On previous days we've seen crocs and hippos in the rivers, but at the moment the only wildlife in view is a pack of hyenas lurking on the opposite shore. It's dark and mercifully cool now, but the heat will be brutal by noon. The smell of fresh bread lures me to the "lodge," a thatched-roof, open-walled structure that houses large stone ovens. Soon Denver and I are seated in safari chairs, ingesting a breakfast of omelettes, coffee, and hot bread.

After breakfast, it's time to prepare ourselves for the hunt. Denver and I spend a few minutes reading from a book titled *Disciplines for the Inner Life*. The themes of today's passages are highly appropriate: anxiety and ungratefulness. They remind me that no matter how apprehensive I am about this day, God is in control, and I must be thankful to Him for simply being here. We are not mighty conquerors come to overpower the savage beast. Instead, we play a role that originated with our forebears, who hunted to sustain themselves, and continues to this day. Something instinctive and God-given has called us here. We are part of the fabric of His creation, men among other living creatures, all threads in His eternal story.

A few minutes later we're gathering our gear and mounting up for a ride in the Land Rover. Besides Denver and me, our party is made up of locals: Isaac, the Zimbabwe game warden; Skumbuzo, the skinner; Polani, the tracker; and Phillip, the professional hunter. Phillip drives, with Isaac beside him. Denver, Skumbuzo, Polani, and I sit on benches in the open back of the Rover.

The sun begins to rise as we bounce along a barely visible path through the bush. Tinted in vibrant orange, a vast landscape emerges around us. Hills and low mountains appear first, followed by tall acacia trees, brown wooded areas dotted with green vegetation, and then rivers and canyons. The area is teeming with wildlife: elephants, zebras, impalas, and many varieties of monkeys. The setting feels serene and deadly at the same time. There is no sign of man.

For the next two hours, we scan the countryside. I think about what may be ahead and practice deep breathing to settle my nerves. Anything could happen today. I want to be calm when it does.

Suddenly, Polani points and calls out, "Over there!" At the same instant, I see them. About a mile away in tall grass are four dark shapes—Cape buffalo.

The Land Rover skids to a halt. Despite my breathing exercises, I can feel my heart begin to race. I pull out binoculars for a better view.

Man, I think. *Look at the horns on that one. Here we go.*

Our team is already dismounting when I reach toward the rack on the back of the truck cab and remove the .375 H&H Magnum I've borrowed from Phillip (I brought my own gun to Africa, a .300 Weatherby, but it's not big enough for Cape buffalo). I check that the magazine is loaded and make sure I have plenty of ammunition. Since I don't know how long I'll be away from the vehicle—it could be minutes or hours—I also grab a backpack filled with water bottles, energy bars, a knife, a jacket, and my Bible. As quietly as possible, I jump to the ground.

It was Saint Irenaeus who once said, "The glory of God is man fully alive." Right now, without doubt, I am fully alive. My senses are on maximum alert. Every bird call and crunch of leaves under my feet seems to echo without end in my brain. I feel each heartbeat inside my chest.

This could be it, I think. *This is my moment.*

I watch the tall grass and the leaves on the trees to check the wind. *Good— it's blowing our way. They won't catch our scent.*

Our team moves to the right, behind the cover of a grass-covered hill and out of sight of the buffalo. Phillip and Polani are whispering to each other and pointing. We're going to keep moving right, around the hill, and hope the small herd is still there when we reach the other side.

The stalk begins. We step in single file, Polani and Phillip in front of me, then Denver, Isaac, and Skumbuzo behind us. Each of us carries a rifle. Periodically, Polani and Phillip stop to "converse," but no words are spoken—all communication is done with hand signals.

It's time to melt into the earth. My attire is designed to make me as invisible as possible: short-sleeved, green and tan polo shirt; khaki pants; and my gray Merrell running shoes. I duck low and steal my way closer to whatever awaits us around the hill.

This is why I hunt, I think. *To get into the rhythm of the land. To sense the sun and wind on my face, to smell the acacia trees, to feel dried leaves and dirt underneath my shoes. There is nothing man-made, nothing artificial here. It's all primitive and pristine—all God.*

Yet even as I revel in the splendor of my circumstances, I'm also acutely aware of how nervous I am. All the efforts of our team are focused on getting me one good shot at the right animal. The success of this venture—maybe even our own well-being—depends on me doing my job.

So many things can go wrong. The herd might detect our scent before I'm ready and stampede—away from us or directly at us. I might have incorrectly sighted my rifle when I tested it in camp. A tree branch or leaf could deflect my shot.

I recall a hunt years before in south Texas. A magnificent mule deer filled my rifle scope. He couldn't have been more than twenty-five yards away. Yet when I pulled the trigger—twice—that deer hightailed it away without even a scratch on him. Somehow, for reasons I've never fathomed, I missed.

And what will happen if I miss this time?

Stop, I think. *It's time to focus.*

After forty-five minutes, we reach the far edge of the hill. Peering over the grass, I see that at least three of the buffalo are still there, grazing. Thankfully, the wind still blows our way.

About ten yards ahead is a downed tree. Phillip points to a spot where a large branch diverts from the trunk—he wants me there.

I nod and ever so slowly creep in that direction.

In a few minutes, we're in position behind the tree. Phillip has a V-shaped shooting stick made from tree branches and thick rubber bands, but we're so close now—maybe thirty yards—that I don't need it. I quietly position the H&H on top of the tree trunk.

Phillip, just a couple of feet away, looks at me and holds up three fingers, then one. Of the three animals we can see, he wants me to go for the closest one.

He's a fine *mbogo,* dark and bulky, with horns that must measure at least eighteen inches between the tips. I can hear those immense jaws pulling and chewing at the grass. I lick my lips and make sure the safety on my H&H is off. I take a sight through the rifle scope and check to see that my shooting lane is clear.

The buffalo moves a couple of steps closer and turns so he's facing us. He's still grazing, still unaware of our presence—so far.

I see movement out of the corner of my eye. Phillip looks at me and extends his palm toward the buffalo: *He's yours, Peb. Whenever you're ready.*

I swallow and take another sight. I can feel the solid, comfortable presence of the weapon in my hands. I'm aware of the sweat beginning to drip down my left cheek and a cramp already forming in my right hamstring. I sense the breeze blowing through the acacias above us and hear the buzz of tsetse flies around me. In my head, I hear my heart pounding harder than before. I imagine I can hear the buffalo's heartbeat too.

I hold still as a statue. I cannot cough or make the slightest sound now. But I must breathe. I force myself to slowly exhale.

The buffalo takes a step forward, then another. He's between two groups of small trees, just twenty-five yards away.

Ever so slightly, I raise the rifle. I center on a spot just below the middle of his chest, right where his heart should be.

Now.

Lord, don't let me miss.

I squeeze the trigger.

I've hunted for almost as long as I can remember. I must have been ten years old when I began taking my first rifle, a .22 Marlin lever-action, out into gray Kansas mornings to stalk "big game" in the evergreen-lined shelter belts designed to stop snow from drifting. In reality, the game was usually squirrels or jack rabbits, but in my mind they were lions, rhinos, or rampaging bull elephants.

For me, the hunt was never about wanting to vanquish another creature. The thrill was simply being out in the elements, be it sun or wind or rain.

I loved storms. I recall awakening at night to the mournful wail of the tornado siren in our little town of Haviland. My father would round up my mother, sister, twin brother, and me, and then we'd all throw on jackets over our pajamas and scurry across the yard to the cellar under the guesthouse. The wind could be fierce, and the cellar, filled with salamanders and fruit jars, was always creepy, but I reveled in the excitement. It was a scene right out of *The Wizard of Oz,* and I was delighted to play it many times.

I remember another scene from my midteens. To earn a few dollars, I was plowing a wheat field for a neighbor. The early morning was beautiful, blue sky as far as I could see, but by late morning a smattering of white clouds had gathered to the west. Over the next few hours, I felt the anticipation build as the clouds grew and darkened. Finally, the sky transformed into an ominous, bulging black mass that filled the heavens, seeming to signal the end of the world.

It was time. I jumped down from the tractor, unhooked the plow, climbed back in, and raced through the darkness at full throttle for the barn two miles away. I didn't make it—the rain attacked with full force, soaking me down to my boots. But I didn't care. I laughed as the storm pummeled me.

It wasn't just inclement weather that triggered this unusual, unrestrained joy. The land itself fascinated me. Twenty miles south of our home was an area called Medicine Lodge, an intriguing territory marked by canyons, streams, and small cliffs. I liked to scramble up and down the rock formations, wander among the cottonwood and juniper trees, and sneak up on deer and coyotes. Spending time in this stimulating environment, so different from the flat Kansas prairies, ignited a passion to see and experience more.

Back then my grandparents lived in Colorado Springs. When we drove across the state line to visit them, my brother, Shel, and I would press our noses against the window of our '57 Chevy, our breath fogging the glass as we competed to see who'd get the first glimpse of Pikes Peak. In our neighborhood, a ten-foot hill was considered a mountain, so Colorado's towering Rockies were almost incomprehensible. That first look at the snowcapped majesty of Pikes Peak never failed to give me a shiver.

I was thirteen when my dad took Shel and me to climb Longs Peak in Rocky Mountain National Park. Though the summit rises to 14,259 feet, the easiest route isn't technical and doesn't require gear. The steep east face of the mountain, on the other hand, can be surmounted only by climbing a deadly sheer cliff known as the Diamond, which features a fifteen-hundred-foot vertical drop.

During a lull on our way up the mountain that day, I crept over to a ledge to catch a glimpse of the east face. I was stunned by what I saw: an enormous, swirling black fog running up, down, and around that impossibly steep terrain. The fog seemed to pulse, as if it were a living creature—one with evil intent.

A couple of hours before, a climber in another group had informed us that two men were taking on the Diamond. Standing there on the ledge, seeing firsthand the water-streaked rock and treacherous fog, I marveled at the thought. *They're out there? In that?* I couldn't imagine what it would take to climb in those conditions—not just the technical know-how, but also the sheer guts to pull it off.

I didn't see how it could be done, yet I desperately wanted to find out. The precipice, both figurative and literal, attracted me. I realized then, as a thirteen-year-old already inclined to take chances, just how much I wanted to challenge myself—to discover my limits and then move beyond them. The lure had been cast, and I was ready to swallow it whole.

Perhaps that helps explain how, over the course of my life, I've found myself exploring trackless territory in the Brooks Range mountains in Alaska; enduring twenty-two hours in subzero weather on avalanche-prone slopes near Aspen, Colorado; contemplating a dangerous river crossing in South America's Patagonia region; and pushing on through a blizzard on a solo ascent of Ben Nevis in Scotland. It provides some hints as to why I've devoted so much energy to climbing, fishing, hunting, sailing, and cycling. It shows, to a degree, why one of my favorite pursuits is spreading out maps to look for a blank spot—and then, when I find one, planning a trip there.

Why, exactly, does that hunger for adventure still rumble in my belly? The challenge is part of it. Every time I journey into the unknown, I learn more about who I am and what I'm capable of. There is nothing like the satisfaction of stepping into the crucible and discovering that, yes, even when mind and body scream that there's nothing left, I *can* keep my grip on an impossibly slim mountain handhold or pedal over the next rise. These discoveries, nuggets mined at the highest altitudes or on the remotest roads, have inspired renewed confidence, motivation, and focus many times thereafter. I've found they deliver encouragement during any trial in life.

The benefits of these risk-laden endeavors go beyond the personal, however. I've learned that the fastest way to deepen a friendship is to enter into an adventure together. There is something about leaving comfort zones behind, surrounding ourselves with God's creation, and meeting obstacles together that strips away pretensions and barriers. It's as if we can't help being "real." We share ideas and experiences that bond us for life. I've seen it happen time and again with families, friends, kids, businessmen, even United Nations diplomats.

One of my dearest buddies is a man twenty years my senior, Orv Mestad. Orv was already a friend before we, along with two companions, decided to climb the east face of California's Mount Whitney. But our experience there cemented a relationship that has lasted more than two decades.

We were about three hundred feet from Whitney's 14,505-foot summit when the mountain unleashed a rock that struck Orv on the head and left him temporarily unconscious. With the day's light nearly gone, going down wasn't an option. I had to hold a bloodied Orv with one hand and, without dropping him into the void below, tie him into a new rope with the other hand so we could ascend the final leg to meet our partners, Dick and Nancy Savidge. Since we'd planned to return by evening and left our overnight gear behind, the four of us huddled in an ice-encased stone hut at the top. Orv was slipping in and out of consciousness, so he rated the lone sleeping bag we'd borrowed from another group of climbers. It was one of the coldest and longest nights of my life.

Dawn, however, brought a welcome change. Orv had improved markedly and was able to descend ahead of us with another climber, a doctor. I'll never forget the memory of meeting Orv at the trailhead five thousand feet below the summit, his head wrapped in a huge bandage, an even bigger smile on his face. "I am so grateful to you guys," he said after embracing each of us. "I feel like I have a new lease on life."

Orv flashed that same smile and gave me another bear hug when I visited him recently at his home in Glendora, California. We've gone climbing and fly-fishing and simply enjoyed each other's company many times since that day on Mount Whitney. There is a bond between us, a brotherhood forged in the mountains years ago, that will never be lost. This deep fellowship that emerged from our shared experience—that always seems to rise up from communal adventure—is one of the great pleasures of my life.

Orv's friendship, and that of many others, has come to mean even more to me recently. My role has changed—once the hunter, I am now the hunted. Through my experience, I've discovered another benefit to living on life's edge, one that overshadows the rest. I've known it for a long time, but I understand it now with crystal clarity.

It was May 12, 2006, when the hunter revealed himself. I was in my office in an old brick building in downtown Colorado Springs. I sat at my oak desk, making phone calls and shuffling papers. A Fernando Ortega CD played in the background.

I was working. But I was also waiting.

A couple of weeks before, a routine blood test had shown that my PSA count was up. Three days earlier, I'd had a biopsy from my prostate. I knew there was potential for something serious. Nevertheless, I wasn't prepared for what I was about to hear.

At 10 a.m., the phone rang. My doctor got right to the point. "Peb, I've got bad news for you. You have cancer. I think you and your wife ought to come over here this afternoon so we can talk about what the next step is."

I hung up the phone. My breathing quickened. I felt a pressure on my forehead. The dreaded word: *cancer.* I could hardly believe it. Only one day earlier I had celebrated my sixty-second birthday. I'd taken care of myself all these years. I felt great, at the top of my game. I was excited about the future.

Suddenly, everything changed.

For a few minutes, I just sat at my desk. The CD kept playing, but I didn't hear it. I wept.

Finally, I began to focus. My eyes took in one of the photos on my wall.

It was a shot by Carl Yarbrough of me cycling on the Dingle Peninsula on Ireland's west coast. Behind me and the single-lane road, the sun was just breaking over the rocky coastline and outlying islands. You couldn't see my expression in the photo, but I knew it was one of pure joy.

A thought ran through my mind: *You know, this isn't a death sentence. They say that if you're going to get cancer, this is the one to get. So, Lord, strengthen me. Give me the courage to face this. I can't put this on the shelf or hide it in a closet. Lord, help me to embrace this experience!*

Over the next few months, that's just what my wife, Sharon, and I did. We talked to doctors. We researched. We learned everything we could about prostate cancer and the treatment options.

I decided on surgery. Doctors removed my prostate on June 19, just a few weeks after the cancer diagnosis. My recovery went well. Additional biopsies uncovered nothing malignant. The prognosis was that I was cancer free and could get on with my life.

Relief.

Then, in mid-August, came an astonishing report: my latest PSA count was nearly identical to presurgery levels. The doctors were so surprised, they ordered a second test. It confirmed the results of the first one.

My cancer was back, and it had spread. An oncologist told me, "It's very likely that it's in your bones. You know that's incurable don't you?"

I had a hard time wrapping my brain around this one. I thought, *Lord, what's going on here? I thought I was free. All of a sudden, I'm not only not free, I've got something lethal.*

Driving home from the hospital, I saw an imaginary neon sign in front of my face. The words that I'd shoved aside before came back to me, flashing on and off, seemingly unavoidable: *death sentence.*

Yet this is where years of pushing myself to the limit began paying dividends. I'd faced perilous situations throughout my life—usually by choice—and had gained so much because of them. Perhaps, I thought, my cancer was less a sentence and more an adventure. Like any good adventure, it was a challenge, a journey into the unknown. It involved a huge element of risk. The stakes were as big as they get. But with the risk would come wonderful side effects: stretching, learning, growing.

And most of all, trusting.

Before any hunt or climb, I do everything I can to prepare myself. I check and pack my gear. I research the area I'm heading to. I plan for multiple scenarios.

I've taken the same approach to living. I've done all I can to ensure a long and enjoyable life. I've eaten well. I've exercised and kept myself in excellent physical condition. And to ward off disease, for years I've taken all the vitamins and supplements designed to prevent maladies such as prostate cancer.

The result? I get one of the most aggressive prostate cancers that exists.

It's helped me realize something: no matter how confident you are in a situation, no matter how much you prepare, no matter how good you are at whatever you do, you're still not in control. Sooner or later everything comes down to dependence on God.

I knew this already. God is Lord of the universe. He's sovereign. He created me and everything around me. My life and the time I have on this earth are entirely in His hands.

But now I *know* it. I understand it with a searing intensity. It's fearful and deeply comforting at the same time. All I have is my trust in Him.

Recently, that trust has taken an interesting turn. To battle my cancer at the physical level, my treatment has included a few months of hormone therapy combined with aggressive diet and supplement programs. But I've also submitted to spiritual "treatments." I've participated in a dozen healing services conducted by friends in Hawaii, San Francisco, my hometown, and elsewhere. These spiritual warriors have traveled from across the country to anoint me with oil, lay hands on me, and pray for my health.

I've done a lot of praying myself. I've talked with God all my life, but my recent experiences with cancer have led to a closeness with Him that I've never felt before.

The apparent outcome of all this surfaced a few months ago in a hospital room in Houston. After a battery of tests, two doctors walked in with befuddled looks on their faces.

"Peb, your situation is very peculiar," one said in an apologetic tone. "We can't find a trace of your cancer."

This was one time I didn't mind being labeled "peculiar." I praised God— once again, I was being pronounced cancer free.

Will I stay that way? I don't know. I'm taking this journey one moment at a time. So I'll continue to value the prayers of friends and will do everything physically and spiritually possible to stay healthy. And I'll cherish every day— every adventure—every perfect moment—that's given me.

What's exciting is that once again I've emerged from the crucible with a new perspective. My life has been burned down to its most basic elements. What remains is my reliance on Him, His sovereignty, and His all-sufficiency.

It is, in fact, all I've ever had.

On that hot day back in the Zimbabwe bush, rifle poised, I'm so focused on the Cape buffalo that I hear nothing when I squeeze the trigger. It's a sublime moment, like a black-and-white photograph, with time silent and frozen.

Abruptly, the moment ends. Sound and color come rushing back.

The buffalo bellows and bucks like a rodeo bull. He kicks up dust and knocks down trees.

I can't believe I missed. "Didn't I hit him? Didn't I hit him?" My voice has jumped an octave, my eyes opened wide.

"You got him good," Phillip says.

The buffalo, enraged, keeps bucking in a circle. His nostrils flare. He doesn't see us. I stare, dumbfounded. I've never seen anything like this.

"If you want, you can take another shot," Phillip says.

I take one long breath to calm my nerves and put another shell into the buffalo. He moans, loud, low, and long.

The buffalo stumbles away. After about twenty yards, he stops and lies down.

Just like that, he's gone.

The emotions converge and wash over me: awe, relief, humility. It is the end of a dream, yet also a beginning, an awakening. I feel I've joined an age-old fellowship inhabited by both man and beast. And as I breathe it all in, the sense of fulfillment is one of the most profound I've ever experienced.

We linger for an hour at the site. I stand near the buffalo's massive body, then sit beside him in the dirt. I touch those deadly horns, saying nothing. It is a privilege to be here. Even the Africans, who have played this scene hundreds of times, speak in reverent whispers.

There is birth, and there is death. In between are the hunter's horn and the brief adventure we call life.

Finally, sweating from the midday heat, we prepare the buffalo for the trip back to camp and pack up our gear. As the truck rolls away, I turn for a last look at the matted brown grass where the *mbogo* lay. Evidence of his presence, and ours, has nearly disappeared; all is silent and still. Yet I can imagine, just on the other side of the hill, his brothers still standing majestically in the veldt, heads high, horns thrust toward the sky and the blazing African sun.

HE IS THERE

I trust in God's unfailing love for ever and ever.
PSALM 52:8

Many years ago I was playing basketball with my friend Jim Dobson and a few other guys in Jim's backyard. It was a typical male-bonding scene filled with trash talking, hard fouls, and plain macho fun. At one point I made a sharp cut to the hoop. My plant didn't hold. I slid to the pavement and writhed in pain, my ankle severely twisted.

The guys, concerned, gathered around me. Jim had his hand on my shoulder. I groaned loudly, my eyes closed. I didn't know how to deal with the sudden agony. Then I opened my eyes and, seeing Jim next to me, shot my right arm out and latched on to his calf with a death grip. I needed something alive, a flesh-and-blood presence, to hold on to. I'll never forget how comforting that felt. Jim's leg was the anchor that got me through a moment of pure anguish.

> *Faith in God is like believing a man can walk over Niagara Falls on a tightrope while pushing a wheelbarrow. Trust in God is like getting in the wheelbarrow!*
> Dr. James Dobson

More times than I can count, I've experienced God's comforting presence in much the same way. During my darkest moments, I've opened my eyes and discovered He is right there. I could grab hold of something indescribable, yet real. The Lord has been with me when I thought I couldn't go on—on remote mountain faces, arduous cycling trails, and raging rivers. And He has certainly journeyed with me during my battle with cancer.

Moses said to the people of Israel, "The LORD himself goes before you and will be with you; he will never leave you nor forsake you" (Deuteronomy 31:8). I believe that promise wholeheartedly.

God will always stand with me. I trust that He's there and that He cares.

Of all the chances I've taken and continue to take in my life, the biggest and most important one is this: I trust God. Jesus put it plainly to the disciples: "Trust in God; trust also in me. In my Father's house are many rooms; if it were not so, I would have told you. I am going there to prepare a place for you" (John 14:1–2).

I want one of those rooms. It's the ultimate destination, the last unexplored territory on the map. I suspect it offers a view of spectacular peaks and quick access to glorious roads and rivers. Yet Jesus makes it clear that to hold my reservation, the required down payment is trust. That's a huge risk, of course. But it's one I'm very willing to take.

> Don't be afraid to go out on a limb. That's where the fruit is.
>
> H. Jackson Browne

—PJ

Remember Leona!

BY JAMES LUND

It's just past dawn when Gil McCormick pops his head out of the snow cave, like a ground squirrel on the first day of spring. The conditions that greet him, however, are anything but springlike. The temperature is ten degrees and thirty-five-mile-an-hour winds lower the windchill to minus fourteen.

Tiny particles of ice immediately begin forming on the tips of Gil's blond beard as he breathes deeply in the thin air. He steps out of the cave into a world most humans would do anything to avoid. He is standing on a precarious ledge carved into a huge mass of overhanging snow. A few feet to the south is a sheer three-thousand-foot drop into Nepal's Khangri Shar Glacier. To the north is a more gradual—but just as deadly—five-thousand-foot decline into Tibet.

But Gil isn't thinking about what lies below. Instead, his gaze takes in hazy blue gray skies and the sweep of Nepal, a spectacular panorama of mountain peaks that includes Cho Oyu, Ama Dablam, and, bathed in an explosion of orange from the sun's first light, the upper flanks of Makalu. Gil McCormick is perched at 22,600 feet on a Himalayan mountain—more than four miles above sea level and higher than any point in North America, Africa, Europe, or Australia.

Gil shivers, but not from the cold or altitude. It's summit day! After months of planning and hassles, after enduring seemingly endless waits for permits to be approved and storms to pass, and after surviving the dangerous climbing of the last few days, Gil and his two companions are ready for the final assault.

He can hardly wait.

Gil looks up. Before him is a stout rock buttress, followed by a long, vertical chute of ice and rock, then a nasty series of rock bands jutting out from the face of the mountain. Beyond that is what appears to be relatively easy climbing to their destination—the snowcapped, near-perfect pyramid that forms the crest of Mount Pumori.

They are less than a thousand feet from completing a new route to the top of a Himalayan peak.

Gil grins. *This wind's a bit brisk, but it's clear—an awesome day for climbing. Praise the Lord! Today we're going to do it!*

The mountains that make up the Himalayas are among God's most inspiring creations, dwarfing the rest of the planet's peaks as an aircraft carrier would a sailboat. The Himalayas extend nearly two thousand miles across eight countries, forming a mighty crescent of unfathomable depth and scope. The range comprises over four hundred 7,000-meter peaks and all fourteen of the world's

8,000-meter mountains, including the tallest of them all at 8,850 meters (29,035 feet)—Everest.

Six miles to the west of Everest, across the Khumbu Glacier and rising out of mist and clouds, is Pumori. Sculpted by thousands of years of sun, ice, and wind, it straddles the border of Tibet and Nepal at a height of 23,493 feet. Pumori, whose name means "daughter mountain" in the Sherpa dialect of the region, was christened by legendary British climber George Mallory—the same man who justified his ambition to scale Everest with the famous phrase "Because it is there!" and who disappeared famously on the slopes of Everest in 1924, apparently short of his goal.*

Everest was eventually conquered to great renown by Sir Edmund Hillary and Tenzing Norgay in 1953, but it wasn't until 1962, when a Swiss-German expedition took on Pumori's southeast face, that mankind left boot prints on the daughter mountain's summit. By the fall of 1990, the time of Gil McCormick's attempt, more than forty expeditions had reached the summit. Nearly all of those climbs were from the south face—the side that faces Everest. No one had summited from the more treacherous northwest ridge, which is where Gil and his two friends find themselves this October morning.

Gil, a twenty-eight-year-old aerospace-industry analyst from Denver, is five feet eleven, 150 pounds, and in the best shape of his life. A powerful, energetic mountaineer, he's been climbing since falling in love with the sport as a junior in high school. This is just his second trip to the Himalayas—and by taking on an unclimbed route, it's his chance to prove his status as one of the world's elite mountaineers.

Gil can barely contain his excitement. Climbing is what makes him feel focused, real, *alive*. The camaraderie, the challenge of facing obstacles and finding out what you're made of—nothing compares to it. Every thought and every moment count. Each day's climb is an adventure, a push into the unknown.

---

* Mallory's body was discovered on a ledge near 27,000 feet in 1999 by the Mallory and Irvine Research Expedition. The expedition found no conclusive evidence that Mallory ever reached the summit.

Even better, in ways he can't fully explain, climbing brings Gil closer to God. He has already experienced some incredible prayer times on Pumori. He prayed for strength, and both of his companions—one a fellow believer, one not—later complimented Gil on his climbing power. He believes God uses his climbing to reveal His glory.

That's what life is all about, isn't it? Gil muses. *To bring glory to God. Not to make summits, to gain power, to make money, to have pleasure. Not unless those things bring glory to Him.*

A figure clad in red and black emerges from the snow cave behind Gil. It is Jim Nowak, a thirty-six-year-old tile craftsman with the physique of a cross-country runner and the strength of a weightlifter. Nowak's climbing credentials include Alaska's Denali, Yosemite's El Capitan, a winter conquest of the Diamond on Longs Peak in Rocky Mountain National Park, and ascents of multiple 20,000-foot peaks in South America. The year before, he and Gil successfully summited 22,500-foot Ama Dablam, about seven miles south of Everest.

Nowak is followed by the official expedition leader, six-foot-one, thirty-five-year-old Steve Van Meter. An accountant, he is calm, focused, and meticulous. It was Van Meter who identified this new route up Pumori's northwest ridge eight years earlier and who planned most of this expedition. Van Meter's background includes ascents of Foraker and the south face of Denali in Alaska. He's led several expeditions in the Himalayas, including Everest, but none have included a summit. Now, with a wife and baby at home in Denver, he knows this could be one of his last chances at a piece of mountaineering history.

It is 5:30 a.m. when the trio begins pulling gear out of the snow cave. It's time to pack up. The plan is to summit by 10:00 that morning, enjoy an hour or so of well-deserved congratulations and photos at the top, and then return to the cave to continue the celebration with a hot tea toast and an early sleep. To enhance speed and mobility, they will carry as little as possible. Sleeping bags and most of the food and equipment will be left behind.

The packing is nearly finished when Van Meter looks up. "What about the stove?" he shouts through the wind.

The question is not an idle one. If the climbers are trapped on or near the summit by a sudden storm—or any other unforeseen development—the portable stove is their only means to generate water.

"Let's bring it," Nowak says. "Just in case."

Gil is thankful for the day's light load. On previous forays up Pumori's face during the three weeks since they left base camp, he has carried as much as eighty pounds on his back. Now his pack contains only two candy bars, a bottle of water, a head lamp, and extra slings.

The pack is so spare, in fact, that Gil wonders if something is missing. Then he remembers.

"Hey, do we have the flags?"

Van Meter looks at Nowak, who shakes his head. "I'll get 'em," Gil says, plunging back into the cave. In moments he discovers the two small flags, one American and one Nepalese. Soon they are nestled at the bottom of Gil's pack, ready for summit photos.

The trio takes only a few minutes to finish strapping on crampons and packs. Gil makes a final check on the tightness of the bright red laces that hold together his Asolo climbing boots.

It's nearly 6 a.m. when Nowak ties into their 160-foot rope at the lead spot. Van Meter ropes up next, followed by Gil. There is no discussion of the order. All three have taken their turns setting the pace during their days on the mountain, particularly Gil and Nowak. Gil, who did the majority of the lead work during the last hard climb two days before, certainly has no objection.

At last the moment they've all anticipated for so long has arrived. It's time to summit. The three men pause to look each other in the eyes.

"This is going to be an exciting day," Van Meter says. "Let's climb strong and be safe."

"Absolutely," Nowak says.

"Let's be careful." Gil says. He adds a silent prayer: *Be with us today, Lord!*

Nowak begins, storming quickly up the buttress and then to the right to traverse a snowy slope toward a large, funnel-like gulley beyond.

Gil, waiting for his turn to climb, feels the familiar rush of exhilaration and adrenaline—along with an unmistakable jolt of fear. *Climbing,* he thinks, *has taught me total reliance on God. Fear drops me to my knees. But I don't fear death, not really, because I know death means eternal life, thanks to Jesus.*

Gil stamps his feet and exhales. Wind instantly snatches away the puff of air that emerges from his lips.

I guess I'm afraid of being taken away from the ones I love, the things of earth, and my mission for God.

Those, and Leona's broken heart.

Leona. The thought of her stabs Gil with a burst of joy and pain. Joy, along with a hint of amazement, at the notion of her presence in his life. Pain at the realization that they have been apart now for five weeks.

They met as students at the University of Colorado, fell in love during a Structural Geology class, and married a year earlier in April. She is everything Gil has ever wanted in a partner—vivacious, spunky, spontaneous, even a bit wild. A woman who exudes unconditional love and acceptance. With long blond hair and brown eyes, she is a true beauty, inside and out.

Before Gil left their home in Denver, Leona handed him a series of "time release" letters to be read during the expedition. Gil opened the last of these at base camp. Even now the memory of her words, uncannily accurate in reading his mood that day and knowing just what encouragement he needed, nearly brings tears to his eyes. He can hardly believe that the Lord has blessed him with the love of such a woman.

Gil doesn't realize that this love, this gift from God, is about to save his life.

Forty-five minutes later, Nowak, still in the lead, has completed his traverse of the slope and gulley. He is at 22,800 feet when he reaches a band of loose rock.

He slows, working efficiently with his ice ax to wade through the dangerous section of shale.

Van Meter waits. He is near the top of the gulley, sixty feet lower and several feet to the left of Nowak's position. He hears Nowak's shout: "I'm at this band! There's going to be some loose stuff coming down!"

The lull in forward progress gives Gil a chance to catch up to Van Meter.

"Hey," Gil says with a grin.

"Hey," Van Meter replies. He looks at Nowak, then to what appears to be a flat ledge at the top of the gulley. It is about fifteen feet up and a few feet to the left. "I think I'll go ahead and climb up to that little ramp."

The angle of the mountain face is forty-five degrees, a relatively easy climb. In moments Van Meter reaches the ledge and disappears from Gil's view.

Despite the favorable climbing conditions, Gil begins to feel uncomfortable about his team's lack of protection. The three are roped together, but no one is attached to the mountain in any way. *You know, this doesn't look real wise. If one of us slips, it could get dicey in a hurry. We could all end up flying down the glacier.*

"Hey, let's get the rack out if we're going to be roped together!" Gil shouts. The "rack" contains their pitons and ice screws, the essential equipment that, after a slip, can mean the difference between remaining in position on the mountain and taking a rapid and final journey to the valleys below.

Gil can't tell if anyone hears him above the wind. With all the layers of clothes and hats over his head and ears, he can barely hear himself. Two days earlier they climbed with helmets, a sensible precaution. Gil still remembers the day he accidentally dropped a rock on a climbing partner in Canada, splitting his helmet and giving him a concussion. The rock was the size of a coffee table; his partner could easily have been killed.

No one is wearing a helmet today, however. Donning a hat, a hood, *and* a helmet just feels too bulky. After all, the climbing from here shouldn't be too difficult.

Still, Gil decides to be as safe as possible. He drives his ice ax deep into the snow, then pulls out a metal spring-loaded device called a Friend. He crams the Friend into a crack in the rock jutting out in front of him and triggers its release. The Friend expands inside the crack, providing Gil with an anchor to clip into.

He looks up, examining the mountain. The path ahead of them appears easy enough. All granite after the first few sections—a definite advantage since mud rock is broken, loose, and hard to find protection in during a rock slide.

Feeling more secure and seeing Nowak still at work above, Gil decides to stay put for now. He lowers his head for a brief rest.

From his ledge above and to the left of Gil, Van Meter watches Nowak make steady progress. A stream of dirt and pebbles falls harmlessly at Van Meter's right into the vastness below.

Suddenly, a small stone about the size of a baseball tumbles down with the scree from Nowak's position. Van Meter immediately hears the shout from above: "Rock!"

In that first instant, Van Meter feels no concern. Nowak's location is well to the right of where he and Gil are positioned.

But the boulder strikes a rock formation and starts a crazy curl to the left. To Van Meter's alarm, it's now headed for a massive snow chute—one aimed directly at the spot where he left Gil.

"Rock!" he yells.

Many climbers are instructed to "tuck in" and cling as close as possible to the mountain during a rock slide. Others, including Gil, have been taught to look up and quickly assess the situation so they can move to one side or another and better protect themselves.

When Gil hears the distant call of "Rock!" he glances up and spies the beginning of the boulder's strange trajectory. He lowers his head and leans into the mountain for perhaps two full seconds.

He believes the rock has passed.

He looks up.

The timing is terribly perfect. Before Gil even has a chance to blink, the boulder smashes directly into the left side of his head, obliterating his prescription sunglasses and the eye behind them. The impact drives him back and nearly off the mountain; he's held in place by the Friend.

Gil feels a surge of pain and screams.

Van Meter, after seeing the freak ricochet of the dislodged boulder and hearing Gil's shriek, scrambles to the lip of the ledge. He spies Gil below, slumped over and holding his left hand awkwardly over his face. His first thought is one of disappointment.

His hand's broken. Oh man, we're not going to make the summit. I can't believe it!

Seeing that there isn't enough slack in the rope between himself and Nowak, Van Meter unties and quickly climbs down to Gil. Gil's face is still covered by his hand.

"How bad is it?" Nowak yells from above.

"Real bad!" Gil shouts back between moans.

Van Meter, realizing it is not a hand injury after all, gently pulls Gil's hand away. He sees a huge gash behind Gil's eye. Tiny shards of glass are embedded in the eye and the area surrounding it. He can see tissue and nerves behind the eyeball. There is blood all around the eye. In warmer conditions, the blood loss would be tremendous, but this high on the mountain, the frigid temperature prevents substantial bleeding.

Peering through his remaining eye, Gil watches Van Meter's face. He has been holding on to a glimmer of hope. The expression that forms as Van Meter examines the eye, however—a mixture of concern, fear, sadness, and compassion—confirms what Gil already suspects. The injury is deadly serious. Gil is filled with an overwhelming sense of failure.

Please, God, let this be a dream. Let everything be okay. We can't lose the summit now. This can't be happening!

"Jim!" Van Meter calls. "You need to come down!"

For even the most careful and professional of climbers, high-altitude mountaineering is a dangerous hobby. People have conquered Everest more than three thousand times since Hillary and Tenzing Norgay, while over two hundred have died in the attempt or on their way down. That's one death for every fifteen successful summits. The ratio is even deadlier for K2, the world's second-highest peak: one fatality for every four summits.

The manner of demise for each victim varies as much as the mountains themselves: avalanche, rock slide, equipment failure, high-altitude sickness, hypothermia, sudden storm—or something as mundane as poor judgment or the tiniest lapse in concentration.

Yet for those who climb, the rewards—some tangible, some not—make the risk worth it. Some of the most skilled earn a living as guides, charging as much as sixty thousand dollars or more to ferry a less-experienced climber to the top of the world. Others make ends meet by working with filmmakers and other commercial expeditions. Still others, such as best-selling author Jon Krakauer, write about their experiences in books and magazines.

Of course, some climbers are merely thrill seekers aiming for a natural high they can't find elsewhere. But most do it because they simply love the sport. They are irresistibly drawn to the mountains in ways they can never fully explain to their families and even to themselves.

For Gil, climbing gives him a sense of purpose and excitement like nothing else can. A successful ascent of a new route on Pumori would open up a new world—invitations to expeditions on the world's tallest and toughest mountains, sponsorships, certainly prestige on an international scale within the climbing community.

And yet, to Gil, it is also something much more. Climbing takes him to a distinctly spiritual place. As he maneuvers one handhold at a time into the clouds, drawing at least symbolically closer to heaven than nearly any other human on the planet, he discovers a deeper connection to his Creator.

In fact, it was Gil's most dangerous climb that crystallized his faith in God.

Gil attended church as a boy, yet God had never seemed real to him. The experience left him unfulfilled. He began searching for answers through science, earning a bachelor's degree in geology in the process. He was still in seeking mode when he decided, along with two climbing friends, to tackle an extremely hazardous route up a 12,000-foot peak near Calgary: Mount Clemenceau.

No one had summited Clemenceau from the north route before. No one had climbed the peak from *any* direction during winter. Gil wanted to do both.

He knew the climb would be greater than any challenge he'd ever faced— that in fact, there was a very reasonable chance he would die in the attempt. His questions about God and faith suddenly took on a new urgency.

He needed to know the truth.

Yet when Gil left his home in Vail, Colorado, for the thirty-six-hour solo drive to Calgary, he still didn't have any answers. He was armed only with his climbing gear, a space heater, and—thanks to his sister—cassette tapes of the entire New Testament.

As he drove, Gil listened to the tapes. All of them. He'd read several books about the Bible before, but this was the first time he'd really explored the actual words of Scripture.

They blew him away.

"I was just overwhelmed with God's love for mankind," Gil says. "I'm sure the Holy Spirit was working on me, moving in my heart. Nothing made more sense. I just got this very real sense of a God who loves His people. I thought, 'Man, this is awesome.' "

Driving again after just two hours of sleep, Gil pulled into Calgary the next evening in a physical and spiritual haze. But he'd come to a decision. After seven years of seeking, he needed to settle up with God. And he needed to do it that night, before taking on Clemenceau.

Near a Walgreens store, Gil found a phone booth and started calling churches and pastors. Eventually he reached a man named Cecil Bailey. "Hey, my name is Gil," he said. "I want to be a Christian and follow Christ. What do I do?"

Though a little taken aback, Bailey invited Gil to his small church.

"He was an old codger in his seventies," Gil says of Bailey. "I don't think he knew what to think of this scraggly hippie from Vail." But during an hour of questions and conversation, Gil convinced Bailey of his sincerity. The pastor introduced Gil to the handful of people who'd braved snow and minus-twenty-degree temperatures to attend the evening service at Bailey's Church of Christ. The pastor related some of Gil's story to the small group of worshipers. And then, in a small chapel on the outskirts of Calgary, Gil was baptized and invited Jesus into his heart for good.

Gil spent the night at Bailey's home. His long spiritual search ended, Gil headed for Clemenceau the next day, feeling "ten million pounds lighter." It was the beginning of a sixteen-day endurance test marked by reconnaissance, waiting out bad weather, and climbing. Gil spent much of those days in prayer, talking with and praising God.

"After all those years of missing Him, I was feeling His presence in a new way, just appreciating His creation and His love," Gil says. "God was talking to me all over the place."

Two weeks later, Gil was ready to plunge even deeper into his relationship with the Lord. Along Clemenceau's northeast ridge, Gil and his two partners discovered an opening to the top. But the team was low on food, and sunset was only two hours away. They faced two thousand feet of difficult ice climbing at a fifty-degree angle. Their only chance of making it before dark would be to shed all excess equipment in order to gain speed.

And they would need to climb without ropes. Without the safety of being linked together, a single slip by any of them would prove fatal. Yet if they turned back, it was unlikely they would ever find a chance to return.

Gil and his partners decided to go for it.

They took off, scaling the ice like spiders on a caffeine overdose, not even stopping for a sip of water. Climbing side by side, ice tools tied into each hand with slings, they fell into an exhilarating rhythm of stretching for the next placement, pulling up, and stretching again. With headlamp beams bouncing off the ice, the trio reached a point just below the summit as darkness and bitter cold closed in. They dug an ice cave, spent the night, scaled Clemenceau's tip the next morning, and then safely descended.

"We pushed the envelope on that climb," Gil says. "That was pretty cool, climbing side by side, knowing that one slip, one mistake, and you're done. For me it was a powerful experience, totally giving myself over to God. It was glorious up there.

"That was my most exciting climb. I never felt so alive."

Twenty minutes after the accident on Pumori, Gil battles a different combination of feelings—adrenaline, shock, despair, guilt. "You guys leave me at the cave. Go on and summit," Gil says as Nowak and Van Meter help him back to the ice cave. "You can pick me up on the way back. I'll be all right." Gil knows the injury is serious, that his eye needs attention as soon as possible, but he feels responsible for the awful turn of events.

"Forget it," Nowak responds. "We're going down. That's all there is to it."

The trio reaches the snow cave. They've already plucked out some of the glass from Gil's eye with tweezers from Van Meter's Swiss Army knife and attempted to clean and bandage the wound. Now Nowak helps Gil through the tiny opening into the coffinlike space they'd carved out hours before. Nowak arranges sleeping bags around Gil in a futile effort to make him comfortable, then crawls out.

Gil is alone. He sits up. "We are so close, Lord!" he shouts. He is overwhelmed by a mixture of anger and pain. Tears fill his eyes while blood drips onto his lap.

It feels like a nightmare. But Gil knows this is no dream.

Lord, he asks, *is this your will? Is* this *your will?*

Nowak returns. "You going to be okay, buddy?"

The pain in Gil's head is intense. "Yeah. I'm all right." He fights off an urge to cry. "I've got some gauze and tape in my bag with the toothbrush."

"Okay. I'll try not to tape your hair, like I did that time on El Cap." Nowak manages a weak grin and searches for the gauze.

Gil can't hold it back any longer. He begins to sob.

Nowak and Gil have been climbing partners for years now and have grown close. They've learned to appreciate each other's strengths as climbers and as men. In the mountains, they've developed an unspoken understanding. When one acts, the other already knows what he's planning and is in agreement. Words are unnecessary.

Now, however, as Gil continues sobbing and Nowak gently replaces the makeshift bandage, Nowak fills in the silence: "I love you, buddy."

Gil sniffles. Nowak's words almost make him feel worse. "I blew it, Jimmy."

"I'm sorry, Gil. I knocked the rock off."

"That's the mountain. It's not your fault."

Nowak finishes taping the bandage and crawls out of the cave without a reply.

On the ledge, Nowak and Van Meter huddle as the wind whips against their down suits. Both are already thinking the same thing: their hope of reaching the summit is gone. The question is, will they be able to get Gil off the mountain?

"How's it look?" Van Meter asks.

"Bad. He's probably going to lose his eye," Nowak says. "If we were any-where else, he'd be in an emergency room."

Van Meter glances toward the snowy summit pyramid, now a bright white against the blue gray sky. "If we went up, he'd be dead by the time we got back."

"I agree."

Both men turn to evaluate the mountain below. It is roughly fifteen hun-dred feet to their tent at Camp II and twice as far to base camp, where the two Sherpas they hired to assist them on this expedition await. The climbers have no radios, no way to contact the Sherpas. Even if they did, no one would be able to mount a credible rescue mission for days.

It is up to the two of them. If they don't get Gil to a doctor quickly—and safely—he will die.

For three strong climbers, the descent would require intense concentra-tion but would not pose any unusual threats. Descending with a man suffer-ing severe head trauma, however, is a dramatically different problem. Gil could easily go into shock, lose consciousness, or develop hypothermia or high-altitude sickness. One slip at the wrong moment could pull them all down. Nowak and Van Meter both know many stories of mountain-rescue attempts that turned tragic.

Time is critical, but first they must make a choice: which way to descend? One option is to rappel down the northwest ridge to the fixed ropes they placed on their way up a day earlier and spend the night at their tent at 21,000 feet. The other choice is to rappel directly down the west face with Gil on a litter, a potentially faster and easier path, all the way to the glacier.

Nowak and Van Meter, both concerned for Gil and fully conscious that the wrong decision could prove fatal, begin a discussion that quickly turns heated.

"We should descend the way we came up—go the way we know," Nowak says.

Van Meter slowly shakes his head. "We don't know if he's going to remain conscious. My guess is he won't. And if he's not conscious, we can't lower him down the ridge."

Nowak frowns. "We've got a limited amount of rock and ice gear. If it runs out in the middle of that face, we're stuck." He shifts his feet, trying to stay warm. "And then we may not be able to get to the tent off the west face. That's a major traverse to the col."

"But on the ridge, there's too many rock formations, too many places where we have to do traverses, too many places where we need Gil to partici-pate. If he goes out, we can't get him down that way and we're in a real bad situation. We should go down the face."

It's Nowak's turn to shake his head. "No way. We wouldn't get down before dark. With a two-hundred-foot rope, that's at least fifteen anchors to place. It's too time consuming. And if we got to the glacier, base camp is, what, another four hours away? And that's for someone—"

"Jim," Van Meter says, his voice rising, "what if Gil checks out? We can't make it down the ridge if he's not helping us. *It can't be done.*"

Nowak takes a deep breath and stares at Van Meter. His words come out hard and measured: "Look. *If* we can keep Gil with us to the fixed ropes, we've got a good chance—a better chance—of getting him safely to the tent and food and shelter. That's the way we need to go."

Van Meter stares back. Then, slowly, his gaze shifts to the ice cave. Gil has crawled out and is sagging against his pack, staring with his right eye into the Himalayan abyss. The bandage over his left eye is red.

For a moment, the only sound is the lonely whistle of the wind.

Van Meter finally turns back to Nowak. "Then we'd better get started."

The descent begins smoothly enough and quickly develops into a routine. Van Meter goes down first with the rope, either climbing or rappelling, and then hammers in two anchors. Nowak begins the delicate task of lowering Gil to Van Meter's position. Gil, roped up and tied into a harness, is essentially forced to walk down the mountain. It's vital that he remain conscious and use his legs—if he doesn't, his body will slam, defenseless, against the rocky ridge.

Once Gil reaches Van Meter, he is clipped into the anchors. Van Meter signals Nowak, and Nowak rappels down to their position. Then Van Meter descends again, and they repeat the procedure.

There is little conversation, other than shouts of encouragement to Gil. Nowak knows they must stay focused if they are to succeed. He feels the tension. Early in the descent, he rappels down to his partners and exchanges glances with Van Meter. *Good.* Nowak is relieved at what he sees in Van Meter's eyes—no sign of anger or resistance, only determination. With the decision on a descent made, both men are committed to working together to rescue their friend.

They make slow but steady progress. By noon, with the sun reflecting off the mountain, the temperature has risen considerably. Yet Gil, even wearing a down jacket, is shivering from cold. Nowak also notices that Gil is contributing less on rappels with his legs.

On Van Meter's next descent, Nowak addresses Gil: "Hey, buddy, tell me your address."

Gil, his right eye closed, moans softly from the pain. "12…780…Dakota Street." The words come out slowly, garbled.

C'mon, Gil, we've got a long way to go. Stay with us!

About an hour later, Gil is sitting in the snow next to Van Meter on a narrow ledge. He has lost most of his sensibilities at this point. At first, he was able to help with his legs during the rappels, and he could hear Van Meter and Nowak shouting to him over the wind and respond. But as the minutes ticked by, he lost focus. His mind wandered. Van Meter's shouts sounded muffled. His frozen legs became more and more useless.

His body, he realizes, is shutting down.

Now Gil's head is still throbbing, but he no longer feels anything from his knees down. He knows that the wind is blowing snow against his face, but he doesn't feel that either. In fact, he's not even cold anymore.

It's the beginning of the end.

He lowers his head to his chest.

I guess this is it, Lord. I'm exhausted. I've got nothing left. I can't move another frozen limb. I am done.

But you know, it's not so bad. I'm ready to go home. I'm at peace. I want *to be with you.*

Head still down, Gil summons the last of his energy and whispers a prayer: "Our Father…who art in heaven…hallowed…be thy name…"

———

Van Meter, next to Gil and working with the rope to bring down Nowak, sees Gil's bowed head and hears him murmuring. He leans closer.

"Thy kingdom come…Thy will be done…"

Van Meter is horrified. *He's giving up. He's making peace with himself. Gil, you can't do this!*

———

Nowak reaches the ledge, sees Gil sitting down and the look on Van Meter's face. "What's wrong?"

"He's saying the Lord's Prayer. He's checking out on us. We're gonna lose this guy."

Nowak's thoughts flash back to weeks before, when he signed a statement requesting that no extreme efforts be made to retrieve his body if he died on the mountain. They'd all signed it. None of them wanted other people risking their lives just to bring their bodies back to civilization. They'd rather have their remains left somewhere high on the mountain. It would be just as well, anyway. They each loved climbing, the breathtaking views, the snow, the air. It would be appropriate.

But at the time, they were just signing a piece of paper. Nowak hadn't really expected it to matter.

He pictures Gil's body encased in ice and snow on the ledge.

Then he imagines the phone call he'd have to make. *Leona, this is Jim. I don't know how to tell you this, but...*

No way.

Nowak storms over to Gil, grabs him by the collar with both gloved hands, and shakes him hard.

"Gil!" he screams against the wind. "Gil!"

No response.

"Gil, get up!"

Again there is no reaction. Then Gil lifts his head slightly. His right eye cracks open.

Nowak, desperate, his face turning red, leans in so close that his nose nearly touches Gil's. "Gil, remember Leona!"

A shudder, perhaps a look of recognition, and maybe something more passes over Gil's face. He blinks. His eye focuses on Nowak's face. He takes a deep breath, then another.

Slowly, Gil raises his right arm to grasp Nowak's left. For a few moments, they are suspended in that position, Gil clutching the lifeline of Nowak's strong left arm. Then, with great effort and with Nowak's help, Gil pulls himself up. The wind continues to whip at Gil's beard and the bandage over his left eye. But he's standing again.

Nowak glances at Van Meter. "Let's go."

Within an hour, Gil begins to improve and is able to participate again in the descent. Utterly spent, the trio reaches the tent at 21,000 feet in the darkness, some thirteen hours after leaving the snow cave that morning.

It is a long night. Nowak and Van Meter pick out more pieces of glass from Gil's eye and rewrap his bandages. Gil throws up everything he takes in, including liquids. Nowak is concerned about the lack of fluid in Gil's body, as well as the possibility of high-altitude pulmonary or cerebral edema. Symptoms of high-altitude sickness include extreme shortness of breath, fatigue, coughing, lack of coordination, hearing or seeing things, and drowsiness. Victims eventually slip into a coma and never wake up.

Nowak and Van Meter take turns watching Gil to make sure he's still breathing. None of them get much sleep, especially Gil, who is still in great pain. But Nowak is thankful to be inside the tent. *At least we've got him out of the wind and weather.*

The next morning, they pack only what they will need for the last descent, leaving most of their gear behind. It takes the climbers only two hours to finish rappelling down to the glacier; from there they can walk to base camp. As they descend to lower and lower altitudes, Gil recovers significantly. On the glacier, he is able to walk without help and stumbles forward at an impressive rate.

My God, he can move on his own, Nowak thinks. *Maybe he's going to make it.*

Soon they encounter the Sherpas, who spotted them descending and came up to assist. With their help, the climbers return to base camp. In case there are any paperwork hassles, it's decided that Van Meter, listed as expedition leader on the government permits, will accompany Gil in the morning on the two-day walk to the town of Lukla, home of the closest airport. Nowak will stay behind with the Sherpas to take care of the gear and break camp.

Nowak is thrilled at the improvement Gil has shown, but when he says good-bye to his friend the next morning, he can't help wondering if he will ever see him again.

As they walk, Van Meter experiences increasing trouble with painful blisters on his feet. Gil, on the other hand, seems physically rejuvenated and actually hikes faster as the morning wears on. He is fueled by emotional turmoil: anger, discouragement, fear for his eye and life. *Why, God?* he prays. *We were so close!*

Where were You up on that mountain? He can't suppress thoughts of bitterness and abandonment. He feels as if he's lost everything.

Late in the morning, they stop. Van Meter's blisters are too painful; he can't keep up. Seeing Gil's determination and knowing his incredible strength, Van Meter reluctantly agrees that Gil should go on alone to the village of Namche Bazaar and then Lukla. It's normally a two-day walk, but Gil will complete the journey in one long day.

On the lonely trek, Gil pops a cassette tape into his portable player. It is a study on the book of Job. Gil's young faith is facing its greatest test; he is reeling physically, emotionally, and spiritually. But as he takes in the breathtaking Nepalese countryside—a glacial river, a wispy fog gently creeping up the valley, the always-dominant Himalayan peaks—and the scriptural account of trials faced by another man so many years ago, he regains a toehold on his slippery faith.

God's words to Job stab Gil in the heart: "Will the one who contends with the Almighty correct him?" (Job 40:2). "Everything under heaven belongs to me" (41:11). Though he can't see any purpose in what has happened, Gil at least considers the possibility that God is still in control, that nothing occurs without His awareness or approval.

When Job replies to God, "Surely I spoke of things I did not understand.… My ears had heard of you but now my eyes have seen you" (42:3, 5), Gil is overwhelmed. He is walking on the same trail as this man Job. He is seeing God like never before.

When Gil hears the end of the book and learns of the increased blessings God heaps on Job, Gil nearly stops in the middle of the trail. *Maybe,* he thinks, *He is still a God of mercy and love.*

Two days later, Gil squirms uncomfortably in a recliner in the family room of his brother's house in Seattle, wearing clean clothes for the first time in weeks and the same eye patch that a doctor gave him at an aid station at 14,000 feet in Nepal. An hour earlier, his brother and sister-in-law picked him up at the airport. In a few minutes, they will rush him to an eye specialist for a hastily arranged appointment.

The incredible stress of the last few days is catching up to Gil. He's dizzy; he feels like he's in a vortex. Everything is moving too fast. He needs something to hang on to, something to stop the spinning.

And then, out of the corner of his good eye, he sees a shape enter the kitchen. Someone is coming.

It is Leona.

There are times in life when the soul-deep mixture of joy, sorrow, and relief cannot be adequately expressed. For Gil, this is one of those moments. He has no words. The tears well up. A knot forms at the back of his throat. He's on his feet. They embrace. "Oh, honey," Leona whispers.

As they stand there with their arms around each other, together again at last, Gil understands that it is only because of this woman, and his love for her, that he is still living.

That and—perhaps—the mercy of a loving God.

FREE AT LAST

> The LORD sets prisoners free, the LORD gives
> sight to the blind.
>
> PSALM 146:7–8

In 1931 Henri Charrière was convicted in Paris of a murder he did not commit, handed a life sentence, and sent to a French penal colony in South America. After repeated unsuccessful escape attempts, the defiant Charrière—also known as Papillon—was sent to the notorious Devil's Island prison in the Caribbean. It had a perfect record; no inmate had ever escaped.

You may not feel much in common with Henri Charrière, a man sentenced to spend the rest of his days on a speck of land surrounded by miles and miles of water. But most of us are trapped in one kind of cell or another. We're stuck in a job we despise. We're held captive by bitterness and an unwillingness to forgive. Once hurt, we're confined by a vow to never let anyone be close again. We're ensnared by addiction. Or materialism. Or feelings of doubt about ourselves and our faith.

All of this is orchestrated by the Evil One: "The thief comes only to steal and kill and destroy" (John 10:10). None of it brings glory to our heavenly Father.

Yet we are governed by a God of love and mercy, not a God of oppression. Our Lord does not wish to see us enslaved by evil. As Jesus said at the synagogue in Nazareth, "He has sent me to proclaim freedom for the prisoners and recovery of sight for the blind" (Luke 4:18).

He's talking about you and me. We are the prisoners. We are the ones in a fog, the ones who cannot see. Through our obedience to His will, God grants us the power to break down the walls of our cells—but He won't do it for us. We must take the initiative to step into risky reliance on Him. If we shut our eyes and ears to God, we're stuck. Unhappy and unwilling to change, we sit in our cells and mark off the days on the wall, month after month, year after year.

And yet God does not give up on us. Part of His mercy is that He will do—or allow—whatever is necessary to prod and push us toward freedom. To open our eyes and point out the way.

In the years since the Pumori summit attempt, Gil McCormick has thought and prayed about his accident many times. He's concluded that the incident was not a random act. They were too near their goal; the strange ricochet of the rock was too accurate; the timing of his last glance upward too timely. His soul tells him that falling rock was a purposeful attack by the Enemy.

Gil knows that he is blessed to still be alive. But his losses that day were real and painful. Despite a year of repeated tests and surgeries, he never regained sight in his left eye. Just as devastating was the end of a life dream.

"Completing a new route up a Himalayan peak is like winning an Olympic gold medal," Gil says. "It would have put me on the cutting edge in the climbing community, set me up for a life of doing this. I already had my path of glory planned out. I had an invitation waiting to climb Everest. It was all right there. Pumori would have launched me."

Instead, because of the issues with his eye, Gil turned down the Everest expedition. He continued to climb, but no longer at an elite level. He struggled and prayed about his faith, asking God, "Why?"—and continued to hear the same answers: *Trust me. Believe in me. Submit to me. Follow me. Depend on me. Step into abundant life with me.*

Slowly, over a period of years, Gil did exactly that. And everything changed for the better.

"Who knows what would have happened to my marriage if I'd continued on that path?" Gil says. "My wife probably would have said, 'I can't take this anymore.' Now I have a great marriage, three great kids, a new career. And I feel closer to God than ever. Those are things climbing can never bring."

He still feels an occasional surge of anger when he thinks about that day on Pumori. Eighteen years later, the northwest route up the "daughter mountain" has yet to be completed by man or woman. But Gil has made peace with the result of the accident and with God. Losing his eye has meant that he sees some things more clearly than ever before. God may not have caused the accident that took Gil's eye and his dream, but He's shown him how to use it for His good purposes. Today, Gil understands the meaning of Paul's words to the Romans like never before: "In *all* things God works for the good of those who love him" (8:28, emphasis added).

> We fix our eyes not on what is seen, but on what is unseen. For what is seen is temporary, but what is unseen is eternal.
>
> 2 Corinthians 4:18

"God knows my weaknesses, what holds me back from His will," Gil says. "He wants to set me free. If there's anything confining any of us, He's going in after it to free us. Going through that process isn't always a pleasant experience. It can be painful to let go of something that doesn't advance the kingdom. But the pain of life is a necessary part of the journey toward utter dependence on God."

Like Henri Charrière—who studied the tides off Devil's Island for months, then jumped off a cliff into the sea at just the right moment and successfully made his escape—Gil knows. Only the greatest risks lead to the greatest rewards: love, freedom, and a life that matters.

—JL

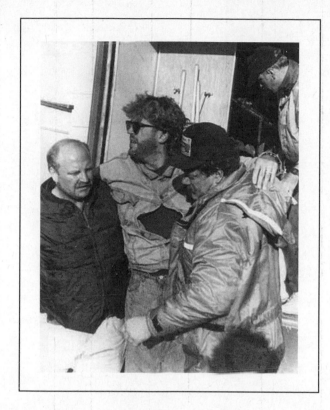

Bering Sea Rescue

BY DAVE ANDERSON WITH NORM ROHRER AND JAMES LUND

On August 14, 1993, a six-member team led by Arizona missionaries Dave Anderson and his wife, Barb, had just completed a visit to Lavrentiya, a remote town on the east coast of Russia. They were ready to go home.

At 2 p.m. that Saturday, we stepped off the tundra of the Russian Far East and climbed aboard Piper Navajo N6SF for the last time. As we strapped in, a gentle wind tugged at our plane and the clouds overhead darkened. My wife,

Barb, shivered and pointed to the fuel gauges standing at what appeared to be a little under half full.

While we waited for takeoff, I thought of the phone call that came two weeks before we left our home in Arizona. A woman named Valerie Bullock had attended one of our concerts and heard about our upcoming mission trip to Russia.

"While you were singing," she said, "I had a vision."

"Of what?" I asked. Something in her voice made me apprehensive.

"Well, I saw your plane fall out of the sky over the ocean near Alaska. You crashed…and…and you all died."

I didn't know what to say. Valerie filled in the silence. "I'm not saying that I know where this vision came from."

I asked if she'd ever had a vision before. "Yes," she said slowly. "And it came true."

Some in our group were already apprehensive about the unknowns of a mission trip to a remote region of Russia. How would we be received? What hardships would we face? What about the language barrier? We also knew that sudden weather changes could easily upset our carefully laid plans. We'd be flying over the capricious, icy waters of the Bering Sea. During the four previous years, more than one hundred commercial fishermen had drowned off the coast of Alaska. No one had ever survived a plane crash into these waters.

Ever.

Yet I sensed that this journey was a risk God wanted us to take. Barb and I had already led successful mission trips to cities and villages in Alaska. When Dick Page, a fellow missionary and pilot, suggested we visit the isolated Russian town of Lavrentiya, it felt like the natural next step. Lavrentiya existed in total spiritual darkness. No one among the population of four thousand had ever seen a church, owned a Bible, or even heard of Jesus Christ. This was the kind of work that excited us most—bringing God's light to the world's darkest places.

I felt God calling us to Lavrentiya. And so we went. I never told anyone, not even Barb, about Valerie's chilling prophecy.

Our time in the Russian Far East was wonderful. We talked, preached, and performed our music. We distributed three thousand pounds of food, one thousand pounds of medical supplies, and five hundred Bibles. Many people opened their hearts to Jesus.

I will never forget the words of Anatoli, a young pharmacy intern: "You say, and you do. I believe what you say because of what you do."

Clearly, God had wanted us to go to Lavrentiya. He was present on the trip, and He was with us still as we prepared for our flight home. I believed nothing would go wrong. Sitting on the plane, I assured Barb that we were in the steady hands of a veteran bush pilot and the Lord. After quick stops in Provideniya on the Russian coast and then Gambell on St. Lawrence Island to have our passports stamped, we would be singing at a concert in Shishmaref, Alaska, before we knew it.

My wife squeezed my hand. I knew she was praying.

At the last minute, pilot Dave Cochran loaded seven empty, blue-and-white, five-gallon Chevron gas cans on board. They would allow him to bring extra fuel to Lavrentiya on his next trip to Russia. I looked at the plane crowded with people, luggage, instruments, and sound equipment and thought, *This is kind of dumb. There's no more room.* I was holding a can in my lap. But then I looked down and saw that the cans would fit exactly in the aisle of the plane.

That'll be okay, I decided.

Dave started the Piper's twin engines. In a few minutes we were rolling—taxiing into position, then streaking down the runway at Lavrentiya, praising God for the wonderful people we had met there. As the nose came up and those powerful engines pulled us toward the sky, we thanked God for the trophies of His grace this trip had provided.

Our pilot banked and headed south toward Provideniya. Halfway through the trip, turbulence struck us full force, tossing the small plane about like a carnival ride. Barb kept her eyes fixed on the instrument panel and prayed. She tried to shake her apprehension, but her fear persisted.

Joining us on the flight was a middle-aged Russian citizen heading back to his home in Alaska. When we landed at Provideniya, he was asked by Russian customs officials to exit the plane. His countrymen determined that his passport was not in order. For nearly an hour, he argued with customs agents who kept making phone calls and huddling in serious discussions. Finally, the Russian informed us, "I have got to get my affairs straightened out. I may need to fly to Moscow. Sorry to have delayed you. Go on ahead without me."

I noticed that Dave had placed ten more blue-and-white gasoline cans, with "Chevron AV Gas" painted on the sides, in the back of the cabin.

Dave taxied the plane to the end of Provideniya's airport. We would be flying by instrument flight rules at seven thousand feet toward St. Lawrence, then Nome. The estimated flying time was one hour and forty-five minutes, and Dave calculated that the plane had fuel in the tanks to spare for the trip home.

Soon Dave opened the throttle, and the seven of us were racing toward the sky once again. I've always been comfortable on airplane flights, so I settled back and quickly fell asleep. Barb, on the other hand, has never enjoyed flying. She kept watching the instrument panel and praying.

Sleet and wind made flying difficult, but the route to St. Lawrence Island was short, and twenty-five minutes later we touched down on a lonesome runway a mile and a half outside Gambell. This tiny Eskimo village on St. Lawrence Island was our official port of entry into the United States. Somehow Dave got the plane leveled off for a landing. We all chuckled when we realized we'd gone back in time—it was Friday the thirteenth again because we'd crossed the International Date Line.

Three men on four-wheel, all-terrain vehicles were waiting at the runway as we taxied up. Dave killed the engines, slid back his window, and yelled above the wind that we needed a U.S. customs agent to stamp our passports.

A few feet from our plane sat another Piper Navajo owned by Bering Air. It was flight 4666, scheduled to take two passengers to Savoonga. Pilot Terry Day was running an hour late that afternoon—a small detail that would have enormous repercussions in the events to follow.

On our plane, Barb leaned over to another member of our team, Pam Swedberg, and whispered that she was afraid we would tip over. *How in the world can we get off the ground in weather like this?* she wondered. *If only those gas gauges would show full.*

The wind continued to blow as the customs agent arrived. He stamped our passports and agreed to make a call to our host in Shishmaref to let him know we would be late for our concert. Our plane rocked and shivered unsteadily as Cary Dietsche, our keyboard player, closed the Piper's door behind the departing customs agent.

Dave throttled up to taxi into position for takeoff. The engines performed flawlessly as the plane rose to its assigned altitude of seven thousand feet, and thankfully several of us were able to sleep.

Barb, however, sat leaning forward in her seat, her eyes fixed on a fuel gauge that continued to edge closer to empty. She remembered Pam saying that the flight to Nome should take only another forty-five minutes and praised God that it would not be much longer. But at the same time, she couldn't shake the feeling that something terrible was about to happen, and she began to call on God for His protection.

At that point, we broke through the clouds into clear blue skies and sunshine. Barb relaxed but still kept her eyes fixed on those gas gauges as they twitched, lower and lower…

Suddenly the right engine coughed. Barb jumped in her seat.

The engine ran for another minute then sputtered again. Calmly Dave switched on a pump to cross feed fuel from the left engine to the right, still convinced he had plenty on board.

The right engine coughed again, and Barb tightened her grip on the seat in front of her. The second hiccup jolted me awake just in time to see the propeller on the right engine slow down, shake unsteadily, then die.

We were in serious trouble.

I heard Dave radio to Nome, "Out of fuel on one tank…descending from seven thousand feet…"

Barb turned her face toward heaven and wept. "If only…"

The voice of the Nome air traffic controller crackled through static: "November Six Sierra Foxtrot, are you declaring an emergency?"

"Yes…please," Dave replied.

"Say how many souls on board."

"Seven."

For some reason the fuel gauges showed one-eighth full, but there was definitely no fuel. Dave radioed Anchorage to tell them he was out of fuel on one engine, had no idea how much fuel was left on the other, and was heading for uninhabited Sledge Island, two-and-a-half miles away.

My mind was racing. Was our glorious mission to Siberia about to end in tragedy? Had Valerie's words been a warning from God that I should have heeded? Had I disobeyed Him by ignoring it?

The vivid memory of her vision was suddenly a cold, evil threat.

We all stared at the dead engine, its propellers now feathered to eliminate drag, trying by prayer and willpower to bring it back to life. The remaining engine purred on.

A few moments later, however, the rhythmic breathing of the Navajo's powerful left engine began to sputter intermittently. Suddenly it, too, went silent.

Dave Cochran later wrote:

"By this time, we were at 3,500 feet and holding at 130 miles per hour, which is about the best glide speed I could get with both props feathered. I was mentally figuring the best way to touch down in the water, as it was obvious we were not going to make it to Sledge Island. I was looking for swells on the water, but there was no pattern, so I elected to land on the same heading that I was now on.

"I was definitely going to leave the landing gear retracted and was trying to decide whether to leave the flaps up or to put them down. Since the flaps would be the first surface to touch the water, the flaps down might cause the airplane to pitch downward, putting more stress on the structure, so I decided to leave the flaps up."

As the nose pitched forward, we all stared at the angry sea. Twenty-three-year-old Brian Brasher, the youngest member of the team and occupant of the seat beside the pilot, was deep in prayer. So was everyone else. There was no panic, even though everybody on board recognized our desperate plight. Each watched in stunned fascination as the rolling sea rushed toward us.

Sea and sky soon blended as the plane sank lower in the air, powerless to rise again. Swirling waves reached up for us as if to snatch us out of the sky.

At first there was only a faint jolt as the fuselage met the tops of the four-foot swells. Dave's white knuckles gripped the steering column as he skillfully held the nose slightly higher than the tail. The plane's fuselage bounced on the waves as its wings cut thin slices of water off the swells, sending plumes into the sky like fountains. Dave struggled to keep the plane from cartwheeling, knowing that it would disintegrate quickly and sink immediately if allowed to hit the water too hard.

Then we struck the surface.

It was like a sledgehammer against rock. A geyser shot straight up, and overstrained joints screamed as the plane bounced along the ocean's surface like a skipped rock. Its nose rose and plunged on the waves like the head of a bucking horse. The plane turned around, then finally stopped, bobbing gently on the surface of the waves. Without a doubt, Dave's expert landing had saved our lives.

"We touched down at about 90 mph and slid along perhaps 300 feet," Cochran wrote. "When I saw a wave building in front of the right wingtip, I tried to lift the wing over it but the wave hit the wingtip and swung the airplane sideways. It stopped and turned 180 degrees from the original heading, with the nose well below the water. It then bobbed up level attitude with water bubbling up through the forward floorboards. I estimated that we had about one and a half minutes to get out of the airplane."

Seawater surged through the plane's floor vents, swirling and sloshing around our feet. Don Wharton, our singer/guitarist, had yanked the lever of the emergency door just before impact. The instant we hit the water, the door ripped away from its hinges and flew off. Cary Dietsche had opened the regular exit door at the same time.

We needed to move fast. I looked at Barb; her foot was caught underneath her seat. She tugged at it frantically. Finally, it pulled free. We headed for the emergency door.

Dave shouted, "Grab a gas can!"

Cary Dietsche had fallen on his knees, stunned. Luggage in the back of the plane had struck his seat with great force, tearing it from its mounts. The rest of us went out the emergency exit and plunged into the dark water, each clinging tightly to an empty five-gallon Chevron gas can. Some of us had two.

Cary made it out the regular door over the wing holding two gas cans. As he stood on the wing, the plane continued to sink. He scrambled to the roof as the plane slowly lowered into the sea. Don, watching from the water, yelled for Cary to jump because the tail was about to strike him. Cary lunged into the sea, and less than a minute later the plane disappeared from view.

We found ourselves in three-to-five-foot swells. The water was near freezing, and only adrenaline prevented us from feeling the full effects of the cold right away.

Despair gnawed at me. Did anyone know where we had gone down? Had anyone seen our crash? How long could anyone remain alive in this bone-numbing water? Fifteen, twenty minutes? Why weren't there life vests aboard? Why not an inflatable raft?

Valerie. God bless her. The vision was coming true, and I hadn't told anyone about it. I was still the only person who knew what was predicted to happen!

In the frigid water we struggled to hang on to the gas cans and shouted encouragement to each other: "Barb, are you okay?" "Don, where are you?" "Cary, are you doing all right?" We called out encouragement from Scripture such as, "No one, not even Satan, can snatch us from God's hands, for we are His children." We quoted psalms and favorite Bible verses.

Brian Brasher kept reminding the group of God's presence, strength, and power. At one point he hollered, "God is our refuge and strength, a very present help in trouble." Later we all heard him shout, "This is the day the Lord has made, let us rejoice and be glad in it."

I thought, *That's the wrong verse.*

The waves were carrying us farther away from each other. I spotted Barb and swam toward her. Finally I caught up with her and was able to grasp a scarf that was wound around her neck. It unwound. She began to float away while I still clutched the scarf. I couldn't seem to follow. I threw the scarf aside. I was angry because my muscles weren't working as they had just minutes before. My body was beginning to shut down.

Our situation was turning beyond desperate.

Yet in our helplessness, things were happening overhead, on shore, and among our families back home. In Amery, Wisconsin, Cary's children had a hard time settling down for bed. They were troubled about their father. His wife gathered them around her for special prayer for their daddy at 11 p.m.— just about the time he was crashing into the Bering Sea.

At the same time, Joan Olson, wife of Mission Aviation Fellowship pilot Dave Olson in Lavrentiya, was also praying for our safety.

Chicago pastor Dave Kyllo was on vacation in Washington State at that time. He later wrote to Barb and me that "for some reason, when we left the house, I picked up your newsletters to read instead of a book…. For two weeks, I felt led to pray especially for my two friends in Christ and their partners in mission. Little did I know what your experiences would be."

Meanwhile, two thousand feet overhead, Bering Air pilot Terry Day had left Gambell with his two passengers, still one hour behind schedule. Out of the corner of his eye, he glimpsed a disturbance on the sea beneath him. The distinct plume of water vanished before he could blink. *Just a whale spouting,* he figured.

A few minutes later a voice on his radio told him that an aircraft had disappeared from radar in the vicinity. The controller asked him to take a look: "Bering Air forty-six sixty-six, I have an aircraft in difficulty that is attempting a landing at Sledge Island. I wonder if it might be possible for you on either a VFR or an IFR clearance to deviate over to the top of Sledge Island on your way to Nome and let me know if you can spot the aircraft on the beach or possibly establish radio contact with him on this frequency or on twenty-one point five."

Day wondered if that spouting he had seen eight or ten minutes earlier could have been our plane crashing into the sea. He rolled his plane into a sharp wingover to get back in a hurry. One of his passengers, an Eskimo woman holding a baby, screamed because she thought the plane was falling out of the sky.

Day scanned the sea. Nothing.

He flew lower, circling the area where he thought he'd seen the whale. "We're over the approximate area, but we can't see anything," Day radioed.

Then Steve Flowers, the other passenger, yelled, "There's a bunch of stuff down there! Go around again."

On the second pass, Steve shouted, "There's people down there!" The Eskimo woman, a Christian from Nome, at once began to pray that each of us would be rescued.

Day told the Nome radio dispatcher that they had spotted survivors of the crash, but that he was running low in fuel and would have to head for Nome. Vic Olson, a pilot with Baker Aviation, was flying another Navajo plane to Shishmaref. He heard the exchange and immediately turned his plane toward Sledge Island. "I've got plenty of fuel and could take over the circling post," he broke in.

"Good," Day responded. "I want someone right here at this spot looking at these folks, or we'll never find them again."

On land, Jay Langton from Nome Flight Service sent word of the crash by telephone to Evergreen Helicopters pilot Eric Penttila, who had just finished dinner with his family in Nome and was about to leave his house. Penttila immediately called his mechanic, Jerry Austin. They bolted from their homes, drove to the hangar, and fired up their large 162 EH helicopter, which was used primarily for food and mail deliveries to isolated villages. It was ill-equipped for rescue but would have to do.

Both men expected to pick up only dead bodies, but they would give it all they had.

A member of the Nome Volunteer Fire Department showed up at the hangar and asked if they could use a firefighter. "I need the strongest, biggest man around," Penttila yelled above the engine.

Soon after, Randy Oles, a tough, broad-shouldered member of the Nome Volunteer Fire Department's search-and-rescue team, grabbed seven body bags, drove to the airport, and jumped in.

By now the helicopter was fully warmed up, filled with fuel, and checked for takeoff.

At about the same time, Era Aviation pilot Walter Greaves and passenger Dave Miles, who were airborne in a helicopter and engaged in a geological survey with a magnetometer, heard the airport frequency reporting that a plane was down. Greaves quickly took stock of his situation. He had an hour and a half of fuel on board. He radioed an offer to help.

"Come!" Penttila responded immediately. Greaves and Miles unhooked and unloaded the cables holding the magnetometer and headed for our site to lend a hand, even though they would be flying illegally over water.

Barb was first to spot the two helicopters approaching on the horizon. She cried out to the rest of us, who were drifting farther and farther apart, but by then we had all seen our salvation approaching in the sky.

The helicopters were both without pontoons and neither had rescue equipment. Yet the men aboard had plenty of dedication and determination. In a few minutes that dedication and determination would be tested as they used all their strength and skills to somehow maneuver between the swells and pluck us from the grips of the unforgiving sea—without letting the back rotor blade touch the water. If the rotor did touch, even for a second, they would have crashed as well, and we all would have died.

The pilots were shocked to find us all alive. They located Brian Brasher first. Eric Penttila lowered his chopper dangerously close to the waves so that Randy Oles could climb out onto the skid to yank Brian from the deep.

But Brian yelled that the injured Cary Dietsche needed to be picked up first. When the rescuers dragged Cary inside, he was suffering severe leg cramps. His fingers, stiff from the cold, were no longer able to grasp the handles of the gas can. He was in the process of letting go when Randy grabbed hold and hauled him up.

"When the helicopters came, they made such a disturbance it forced you and your can underwater," Cary said. "You couldn't see or breathe. Randy tapped me on the head and said, 'Let's go.' I was so numb that I couldn't help him get me into the helicopter."

Finally, forty minutes after our crash, one of us had escaped the chilling grip of the Bering Sea.

The Evergreen crew headed next for me. I yelled for them to pick up Barb, but the rescuers couldn't hear amidst the incredible noise of the swirling blades and the tremendous spray of water they created.

Randy Oles again climbed out onto the skid and grabbed my hand. But my strength was gone, and my clothing was soaked with seawater, increasing my weight. Oles could not pull me up by himself. It was a tense situation.

Then the skid of the helicopter momentarily dipped beneath the water. I was able to slide my right leg over the skid and gain some leverage. Oles grabbed my belt and pulled me in.

Nearby, Dave Cochran was drifting in and out of consciousness. He had lost his grip on his gas can and was floating free, sinking lower and lower into the water. His heavy coat was soaked, making it difficult to pull him in.

By this time the two rescuers were nearly exhausted. Both Randy Oles and Jerry Austin were outside the helicopter on the skid trying to make contact with Dave. In a final effort, they threw the ends of a rope inside to Cary and me. With what little strength we had left, we pulled the rope tight and hung on. Austin and Oles slid out farther and farther on the skid, finally getting Dave in their grip.

Before Dave was even on board, Penttila took off for Sledge Island.

The small island, a craggy outpost of rock and tundra, offered only one landing spot—a plateau more than sixteen stories high. Oles and Austin literally held Cochran in midair on the skid until he was deposited on top of the island.

After the helicopter landed, Cary Dietsche and I crawled out and covered the seventy-year-old pilot with a sleeping bag as Penttila took off again. Cary and I tried to give Dave a bit of warmth and make him as comfortable as possible. We had to slap his face to keep him from slipping into unconsciousness. We called out things like, "Hold on, Dave… We're going to make it… We're on top of the island… They've gone for the others."

While all of this was taking place, Terry Day of Bering Air had unloaded his passengers in Nome, refueled, and returned to position himself in a circling pattern halfway between Nome and Sledge Island. From there he relayed information by radio to Nome.

Meanwhile, Walter Greaves and Dave Miles were having trouble plucking Barb from the water. Miles was able to grab her and keep her from sinking, but her clothing was so heavy he couldn't lift her into the helicopter. She was too weak to hold on to anything, and the swells made it difficult for the pilot to hover. When the waves crested and the troughs were low, the helicopter dropped closer to Barb; when the waves fell—sometimes as much as six feet—the helicopter couldn't follow because the tail rotor might hit the wave and cause a disaster.

The frustrated rescuers were growing desperate. They finally decided they had to leave Barb momentarily but couldn't bring themselves to do it. They were pretty sure she would drown because she had let go of her gas can while preparing to be raised into the helicopter.

On one final, valiant try, Miles, a thirty-year-old Canadian who later received the American Medal of Heroism for his efforts, hung on to a black strap anchored to the helicopter and eased himself out farther and farther on the skid. He was able to grab Barb with his free hand but then felt his grip on the strap weakening. So he let go of it, and with one last mighty effort grabbed Barb with both hands. He locked her head between his knees and wrapped his legs around her chest as he clung to the skid with his arms.

Greaves gently lifted off the water and headed for Sledge Island, flying low above the waves as Miles struggled to maintain his grip on the helicopter skid while Barb dangled beneath him. They flew in this precarious position for nearly two miles.

As they neared Sledge Island's rocky shore and began to rise to the plateau, Miles felt Barb begin to slip out of his leg lock. "Go down! Go down!" he yelled at Greaves. "She's slipping!"

Pausing a few feet from shore, Miles reluctantly dropped Barbara back into the water. She was terrified.

Oh, God, she prayed, *help me to surface; my strength is gone!* As she pushed herself upward, her breath escaped, and with one final thrust toward the surface, she inhaled. Her lungs filled with water. She gasped and choked in an effort to breathe fresh air.

Finally Barb prayed to the Lord again, but with a different request: *Let me pass into your arms of comfort.*

Dave Miles stood in the helicopter doorway, feeling useless. Below him, Barb cried out, "Help me—help me—can't you see I'm drowning?"

Frustrated and desperately searching for a way to help, Greaves took the helicopter higher. It disappeared from Barb's view.

Exhausted, Barb lay back in the water as if it were a comfortable feather bed. *Jesus…Jesus…help…help…* she whimpered. The rhythm of the plea was like a lullaby. Her anxiety disappeared. God gave her an overwhelming peace…to die.

"You can make it! Come to me." The voice pierced the air. Barb awoke into full consciousness. *Is this a voice behind me?* she thought. She turned in the water. Dave Miles was standing near the rocks in the water.

You can make it! Barb thought. *Have I been lying here dying all this time, and I could have walked to shore?*

Barb placed her feet downward, searching for solid ground. She stood, took a step forward, and fell again into the water. She tried to swim. Miles made his way toward her, shouting words of encouragement. He grabbed her and dragged her to a rock where they sat down. He massaged Barb's trembling hands and removed her drenched coat from her shaking body to allow her clothing to absorb the heat of the sun, even though the temperature on that mid-August day was only forty-two degrees.

During Barb's dramatic helicopter rescue, Don Wharton and Pam Swedberg were rescued by Eric Penttila's team. Pam was able to get into the helicopter, but Don was not. His rescuers held on to him as he dangled on the skid of the helicopter while they flew to the top of the island to join the rest of us.

Greaves made the final trip to the crash site to pick up Brian Brasher, the last to be rescued. The sun was in the pilot's eyes, and he had difficulty finding Brian. There were about a dozen five-gallon gas cans floating on the surface by then, scattered over six hundred feet, and the Evergreen crew thought mistakenly that Brian would be with the others. His gas can was under water, making it even harder to locate him.

In the sea, Brian experienced a surge of fear as the pilot flew over him four times without seeing him. He could have been the first to be rescued had he not insisted that the helicopters get Cary. The young Christian teacher was close to giving up and yielding to the effects of hypothermia because the helicopters had not returned for about fifteen minutes.

"I actually felt Satan's tug," Brian says. "We'd been over in Russia doing God's work, honoring Him, and now Satan was going to get us back. I felt him trying to pull me into the water."

Greaves finally located Brian, but since he was alone in the craft, he hovered over the young man until Eric Penttila and his team could return and fish Brian out of the sea. He had been in the water for seventy minutes. With Brian on board, Penttila flew to the base of the island along the shore, picked up Barb and Dave Miles, then delivered them to the mountaintop where they joined the rest of us.

Penttila radioed the airport and asked for ambulances to be ready to take his wet, exhausted, and trembling passengers straight to the emergency room. He needn't have bothered. The whole town was mobilized already, eager to help their "neighbors."

I was put onto corrugated metal in the helicopter freight compartment with Cary and Pam Swedberg, but Cary was claustrophobic and had to be taken out. Dave Miles took his place. En route to Nome we struggled just to remain conscious, shivering uncontrollably.

Ambulances had raced to the airport and were waiting. The prayer rooms of churches began filling up. Pastors Marv Eppard, Bill Welch, Jim Falsey, and several other men of the cloth rushed to the Norton Sound Regional Hospital, where nurses, doctors, and other attendants were gathered to be on hand when the victims arrived. Townspeople brought dry clothing for the survivors.

The Christian woman aboard Bering Air's flight 4666 when we were first spotted in the water was there too, weeping for joy and thanking God for doing the impossible. In English and in her Eskimo language, she continued to pray in the hospital for God to bless us with a complete recovery.

Even as the helicopters were settling on the tarmac, the seven of us who had just been plucked from the sea were all still so cold we were shaking uncontrollably. A specialist in preventive medicine, Dr. David Arday, later told me we were "clearly in the 'marginal zone' of survivability out there on the Bering Sea, which begins at fifteen to thirty minutes—especially given the wind and waves." The arrival of the rescue helicopters, Dr. Arday believes, provided enough stimulation to keep our adrenaline up, which helped us to maintain the will to live. It kept us conscious and kept us shivering.

Believe me, we did a lot of that!

We were all very close to having a core temperature below ninety degrees, which constitutes severe hypothermia. Some of us were minutes away from coma and possibly cardiopulmonary arrest, which would have caused us to appear clinically dead.

The hospital staff in Nome knew all this and was ready for action when the two ambulances arrived. Each of us was rushed to a warm room, put to bed, wrapped in warm blankets, and readied for examination. Two or three attendants were at every bedside. They cut off our salty clothing, massaged our limbs to restore circulation, and fed us hot beverages and food. A few minutes longer and hypothermia would have claimed the lives of most, if not all, of us.

Maurice Ninham, administrator of Norton Sound Regional Hospital, had just recently read the hospital's disaster-drill manual and was prepared to deal with the press. During the lengthening evening, he presented routine statements concerning the condition of the victims and cooperated with Pastor Eppard in finding places for us to spend the night when we were released. Barb and Dave Cochran were kept overnight for extended treatment and observation.

In the midst of all the activity at the hospital that evening, a baby girl was born. You could say that all of us were given a fresh start on life that eventful day.

Somehow, we had made it.

The next day, Cary, Don, and Brian caught flights to their hometowns in the States. Dave Cochran and Pam Swedberg returned to their homes in Soldotna, on Alaska's Kenai Peninsula.

As for Barb and me, our tickets home were at the bottom of the sea. Alaska Airlines graciously reissued our tickets and upgraded us to first class. All the flight personnel knew what we had been through. There were a lot of tears and tender hearts as we rehearsed how differently the story might have ended.

As a courtesy, the pilot of our jetliner made a long turn out of Nome in the opposite direction from the usual flight plan so that he could use his special camera mounted in the cockpit to take a photograph of Sledge Island for our memory book. Looking down on what could have been our grave is an experience I will never forget.

What about Valerie's vision of death? What was its significance?

I don't know the answer for certain. But I believe the crash and rescue once again demonstrate the sovereignty of God. They bring to life the words of Scripture: "He rescues and he saves; he performs signs and wonders in the heavens and on the earth" (Daniel 6:27).

God is in control. I am not. When I give up, He doesn't. When my strength is gone, His isn't. When there is no hope, He is there. He is a God of the impossible.

"'COURSE HE ISN'T SAFE"

> Who shall separate us from the love of Christ?
> Shall trouble or hardship or persecution or
> famine or nakedness or danger or sword? As
> it is written: "For your sake we face death all
> day long."
>
> ROMANS 8:35–36

You probably know this conversation from C. S. Lewis's classic fantasy series, The Chronicles of Narnia. A group of children and beavers are discussing a lion named Aslan when one of the children speaks:

"Is he—quite safe? I shall feel rather nervous about meeting a lion."

"That you will, dearie, and no mistake," said Mrs. Beaver; "if there's anyone who can appear before Aslan without their knees knocking, they're either braver than most or else just silly."

"Then he isn't safe?" said Lucy.

"Safe?" said Mr. Beaver; "don't you hear what Mrs. Beaver tells you? Who said anything about safe? 'Course he isn't safe. But he's good. He's the King, I tell you."

Lewis's characters may be referring to a lion, but most people believe Lewis is really talking about God. A God of infinite power. A God of unfathomable mystery. A God who exists beyond our understanding of time and space.

A God who isn't at all safe.

I don't know about you, but I prefer to dwell on our heavenly Father's most comforting—and comfortable—qualities. I am warmed to the core of my being by the fact that He loves me personally (see 1 John 4:15–16). I draw strength from His commitment to peace and order (see 1 Corinthians 14:33, 40). I am relieved by the knowledge that He will protect me in times of trouble (see Psalm 32:7).

I could mediate for weeks at a time on these aspects of God. They are my anchor. They leave me feeling serene and secure.

But God offers more than this. Much more.

If we want to experience everything that God extends to us—if we desire the full measure of His intended blessings for each of us— we must embrace *all* of Him. We must follow Him persistently and completely. Not just when it's convenient. Not only when it's comfortable.

When God emerges from the mist and crooks His finger at us, it is not time to shrink back or turn away. This is the moment to step boldly forward. We are like Indiana Jones at the mouth of a dark, twisting, underground tunnel. We know an incredible treasure is down there, just waiting to be discovered. But we also know there's danger ahead. Traps. Natives with spears. Many, many snakes.

Dave Anderson found himself at the mouth of such a tunnel. He sensed God's invitation to step inside and bring light to the people of Lavrentiya. But first He had to confront a vision—a frightening warning of death.

The Enemy is like that. He has a way of appearing just when we are about to do the greatest good.

Dave chose to ignore the warning and answer the call of God. Fully aware of the risk, he stepped into the tunnel.

So what will you do when God beckons?

If you choose to enter the tunnel, you must travel light. Your only supplies will be your faith and a dim torch. Yet they are enough. It's true that God won't lead you by the hand or give you an easy-reference map to His treasure of blessings. But He will "throw a beam of light" (Psalm 119:105, MSG) to reveal your next step. And if you take that step, He'll provide just enough light to see the one after that.

Yes, there is risk in going forward. Yes, it is dangerous.

Yes, in some situations, it's even possible that you could die. Dave and his team almost did. If not for a string of "impossible" coincidences and the courage, skill, and dedication of their rescuers, their bodies would be resting at the bottom of the Bering Sea today.

But honestly, what is the better choice—to live timidly, only capturing fleeting and unsatisfying glimpses on the horizon of God's shining glory, or to seize boldly the treasure that God offers, even if it may lead to death, knowing that we rest completely in His loving embrace? Wasn't it Paul who said, "To live is Christ and to die is gain" (Philippians 1:21)?

> Faith is a living, daring confidence in God's grace, so sure and certain that the believer would stake his life on it a thousand times.
>
> Martin Luther

Dave Anderson seized the treasure. He experienced not just the joy of seeing Lavrentiya's people come to know their Lord but also a deepening of his own faith.

"Since the rescue, I have encountered a number of 'this is way too much for me' events," he says. "My response has usually been, 'If the Lord could save us from the Bering Sea, He can easily handle this one.' I know that God is in control.

"I don't know much about the future. But I know who holds the future, and I'm trusting in His guidance."

Risk only for the sake of risk is foolhardy. It's a meaningless gesture, a search for cheap thrills.

But risk when it's a response to the call of God is another matter entirely. It's exactly where you and I need to be. And it reveals that wonderful paradox: God may not be safe, but risking for God is actually no risk at all. It's drawing near to the safest place we'll ever find.

—JL

Guardian Angel

BY JAMES LUND

Tuesday, 5:35 a.m.
Interstate 395, Arlington, Virginia

With stars still visible in the cloudless predawn sky, U.S. Army Ranger Sgt. Christopher Braman accelerates past highway traffic in his Jeep Wrangler. He has a full morning ahead, and he wants to reach his office as quickly as possible. His destination is a five-story, five-sided monolith near the Potomac River: the Pentagon.

In the movie *Under Siege,* Steven Seagal plays a cook who is an ex-Navy SEAL. Braman is the Rangers' version of Seagal. The thirty-three-year-old is working on a degree in hotel/motel management and nutrition and has served for two years at the Secretary of the Army General Officers' Mess as a cook and purchasing agent. But his skills range far beyond the kitchen. He's also trained in rifle and automatic weapons marksmanship, jiujitsu, combat search and rescue, demolitions, parachuting, and water operations and has acted as an instructor of most of those. He's seen combat in Iraq, Turkey, and Macedonia and earned more than a dozen medals for his performance on the battlefield.

Chris Braman may be the most dangerous cook in the world, with an attitude to match his abilities. He's a man you don't want to cross. When he suspected a few months earlier that his neighbor, Rick, had used a Taser gun on his dog and then lied about it, Braman confronted him. "If I ever find out that you hurt my dog," he told his neighbor, "I'm going to rip your throat out and feed it to your wife."

Braman isn't expecting any confrontations today. His mission is to help prepare for a lunch meeting for army generals and members of Congress. He mentally ticks off the menu items he'll need to track down in the D.C. area for Sgt. Wise, the "GOMess" executive chef: wine, trout, blue crab, a sheet cake, and a host of ingredients.

This, he thinks as he pulls into the south parking lot at the Pentagon, *will be a busy morning.*

It is September 11, 2001.

5:50 a.m.
Union Station, Washington, D.C.

Wearing a khaki suit jacket, Sheila Moody stands before a color-coded Metro subway map and tries to calculate an efficient route to work. She's about to start her second day in a new job as an accountant at the Pentagon. It'll be her first day, really, because she spent yesterday filling out paperwork and taking a tour. Her initial stop Monday was at a personnel office in Virginia, so this is her first attempt to reach the Pentagon from Union Station.

Forty-two years old, Moody is the wife of a former soldier and mother of two college students and a son in high school, all still in New York. Her husband, son, and mother, who lives with Moody and her family, will follow her to the D.C. area as soon as they can.

Born in nearby Severn, Maryland, Moody has worked for the army most of her adult life. Her first job out of high school was as a clerk-typist at Maryland's Fort Meade. She spent the past six years with an army finance office in Rome, New York, before applying for her new job at the Pentagon. She's excited about the change. It's a chance to move back to the region she grew up in, return to a church she loves, and work in one of the world's most fascinating places.

At the moment, however, as Moody stares at the subway map, she's feeling closer to confused than excited. There are so many options. Yesterday was the first time she'd been on a commuter or subway train in her life. It's a bit overwhelming.

Moody almost chose not to come in today. She missed an appointment the day before with the government-contracted housing office that is supposed to provide her with a temporary apartment. But she decided it would be best to report for work this morning and take care of her housing in the afternoon.

Suddenly, in the sea of faces passing behind the map, Moody recognizes one. *I know him,* she thinks. *I met him yesterday in the office at the Pentagon. I'll just follow him and see where he goes.*

When the man enters one of the trains, Moody lines up behind him and sits down several feet away. She exhales in relief. She is where she's supposed to be.

8:20 a.m.
Dulles International Airport, Dulles, Virginia

Ten minutes behind schedule, an American Airlines Boeing 757 roars down the runway. The pilot pulls up on the throttle, easing the jet into the sky.

Flight 77, bound for Los Angeles, carries fifty-eight passengers and six crew members.

In First Class, sitting in seat 1B, is twenty-nine-year-old Hani Hanjour. Born in Saudi Arabia and recently a resident of Paterson, New Jersey, Hanjour earned a commercial pilot's license two years ago. His license has since expired.

8:25 a.m.
General Officers' Mess, C Wing, the Pentagon

Chris Braman is loading supplies off an electric cart into his third-floor office, which also serves as a storeroom. Within the last two hours, he's been to a wine shop in Maryland, the wharf in D.C., a Virginia grocery store, and a nearby German bakery.

Wise, the GOMess chef, pokes his head through the doorway. "Hey, Ranger, where you been? I needed that stuff two hours ago."

Wise, Braman thinks, *always needs it two hours ago.* "You can't stress me," the Ranger replies. "Shut up. Go do some push-ups." He smiles as he says the words, but the exchange is typical of Braman's people interactions. Even when he's projecting an easygoing exterior, he finds ways to keep anyone from getting too close—including his wife and three daughters.

Braman grew up in Mission Viejo, California, but hardly resembled the stereotype of the laid-back, SoCal surfer dude. It had to do with his family legacy. Braman's father was in the U.S. Navy Reserve; one grandfather was a navy hero during World War II, and the other fought in the army. Nearly everyone in the family served the country in the military, on a police force, or in some other profession. Braman was proud of that legacy and had every intention of continuing it.

While in junior college, Braman enlisted in the army. He planned to be the best, registered for Ranger school, and made it. He wanted to see Europe, so he signed up for an opening as an infantry cook. His first deployment was in Germany, where he watched the Berlin Wall come down. That was followed by combat during Desert Storm and the Bosnia-Herzegovina conflict. He took culinary classes. He took military classes. He trained incessantly. Somewhere during those eleven years, he found time to get married and start a family, yet his motto remained the same: "Work is my hobby."

For a long time, Braman and his family have dealt with an invisible wall of separation. It hasn't helped, of course, that he's so frequently deployed overseas. But there is a divide even when he's home. For example, he'd attended church regularly as a child and had always had a strong faith. Yet for years his wife, Samaria, and their kids went to church without him. Braman was too focused on work, too absorbed in training. Just last Easter he finally decided that if his family was going to worship every week, maybe he needed to be there with them.

Braman's Ranger training included practice at a firing range filled with pop-up rubber mannequins. Some of the mannequins held harmless objects such as an electric shaver. Others held weapons. Braman's task was to instantly identify whether or not the mannequin was a threat, shoot when appropriate, then move on.

He mastered the exercise. It became his modus operandi on the battlefield. All too often, it was also his approach to life.

In his office/storeroom, Braman has already worked up a sweat. He wants to finish unloading the boxes and get his purchases entered on the computer before his morning staff meeting.

8:45 a.m.
E Wing Corridor, the Pentagon

Walking rapidly, Sheila Moody swivels her head back and forth, trying to take it all in. She's in one of the fifteen-foot-wide hallways that extend throughout the Pentagon. It's crowded with army, navy, air force, and marine personnel, all moving with purpose. *This place is huge,* she thinks. *There are so many people.*

Everybody seems to know where they're going except me. Moody weaves left to dodge a maintenance man on a golf cart.

Though she has no idea where it is, Moody is on her way to the Department of Defense payroll office to turn in paperwork. She's accompanied by Louise Kurtz, who's already been there. Moody met Kurtz the day before and was surprised to learn that not only is she, like Moody, starting a new job in the same Pentagon department, but also that Kurtz used to be stationed at an air force base in Rome.

Moody is relieved to have so quickly found a friend. She isn't sure how she'd get through the morning otherwise.

8:47 a.m.
Indianapolis Control Center, Indianapolis, Indiana

A flight controller in Indianapolis advises the pilots of Flight 77 on their course. "American seventy-seven, turn ten degrees to the right vectors for traffic," the controller radios.

"Ten right, American seven-seven," responds a pilot.

Three minutes later, Indianapolis Control sends another message: "American seventy-seven cleared direct, ah, Falmouth."

"Ah, direct Falmouth, American seventy-seven, thanks," is the immediate answer. The pilot's voice is calm.

Six minutes pass. At 8:56 a.m., the controller is back on the radio: "American seventy-seven, Indy."

The controller waits a few seconds. There is no response.

"American seventy-seven, Indy," he says again.

Still no answer.

"American seventy-seven, Indy," he says for the third time. "American, seventy-seven American, Indy radio check. How do you read?" The controller listens for fifteen seconds, then tries again. "American, ah, seventy-seven American, radio check. How do you read?"

Silence. The controller stares at his microphone.

9:33 a.m.
General Officers' Mess, C Wing, the Pentagon

Chris Braman has finished entering all of his morning purchases on his computer. Now he's eating a bowl of raisin bran at his desk. The phone rings.

"Chris?" It's Samaria. Her voice sounds shaky. Their youngest daughter, Miranda, must be watching a video; Braman can hear a Veggie Tales song in the background.

"Yeah, hon," he says.

"Your dad just called. He says somebody hijacked a jet and crashed it into the Twin Towers in New York—"

"Okay. You know, this morning I was just reading about this guy, a general in Afghanistan, who was assassinated."

"Chris. They're saying it's possible that D.C. could be next."

This time the news sinks in. Braman begins typing the address for the CNN Web site on his computer.

"Honey, not to worry," he says. "I gotta go. I love you."

Braman hangs up the phone.

He hears, from somewhere outside, a strange *whoosh* sound.

9:34 a.m.
Office 1E-472, E Wing, the Pentagon

Sheila Moody is in her new cubicle, the first in the row of cubicles in her first-floor office. If she stands, she can see a parking lot through the window at the far end of the office. Right now, though, she's sitting at her desk. Except for her computer, the desk is bare; most of Moody's personal effects are still in New York with her family. Today all she has with her is a Palm Pilot, a novel to read at lunch, and a Bible. She's still wearing the suit jacket she had on when she arrived.

Moody types an e-mail message to her former co-workers in Rome: "I miss you guys. This place is huge. I feel like a small fish in a big pond."

Louise Kurtz, holding a sheaf of papers, appears at the entrance to Moody's cubicle. She has an odd expression on her face.

"Sheila," she says. "I just heard on the radio that two planes crashed into the World Trade Center. They think it's terrorists."

"What?" Moody's eyes widen. "That's…unbelievable."

"I know. I know."

Kurtz turns away and walks toward the fax machine near the window. Moody, stunned by the news, turns back to her desk.

A sound that makes no sense—the noise a jet makes as it's landing—interrupts Moody's thoughts.

The noise abruptly transforms into the sound of a deafening explosion. Everything in the cubicle, including the floor, begins to shake. A blast of heat strikes Moody in the face; she closes her eyes. When she opens them, an orange fireball is shooting past in the same spot Kurtz stood moments before, so close Moody could extend her arm and touch it. Later she is told that temperatures inside the Pentagon reached sixteen hundred degrees that morning.

This isn't what Moody expected her first day on the job. Her first coherent thought is, *What kind of place is this?*

9:37 a.m.
General Officers' Mess, C Wing, the Pentagon

Chris Braman, sitting at his desk trying to identify the strange noise, is suddenly thrown to his left. He slams into a row of white wooden cabinets. He lands on his feet.

For Braman, the impact is like flipping a switch. Adrenaline surges through his five-foot-ten frame. He doesn't know what's happening, but this is a time to act, not analyze. Braman is instantly in combat mode.

The Ranger-cook scrambles into the hallway. The building is shaking. Water is seeping through cracks in the ceiling. Smoke is flooding everywhere. People are running for the stairs. "Get out, get out, get out!" he yells.

Wise appears next to him. The chef runs to the right, Braman to the left. On the stairs, a Department of Defense police officer is carrying a woman and her baby. Braman helps the officer. The back of the baby's hair is singed. The woman is covered with ash and can't see. She cries over and over, "Where is my baby?"

Braman and the officer reach the bottom of the stairs, throw open a door, and burst into sunlight. Braman and the officer carry the woman and child about fifty feet across the lawn in front of the Pentagon's west face, then lay them down in the grass. Braman places the baby in the woman's arms.

The officer locks eyes with Braman. "Go get help," Braman says.

9:38 a.m.
Office 1E-472, E Wing, the Pentagon

Still sitting down, in shock, Sheila Moody hears screams from close by. Suddenly, burnt ceiling tiles fall, landing on her hands. Moody stands and shakes off the embers. Her hands hurt. Her back is incredibly hot; she takes off her jacket.

She is surrounded by thick black smoke and orange flames just two feet away. She can't see anything else. *Which way is the exit?* She can't remember.

Moody turns and makes out a window near the ceiling. She steps through fire, climbs onto a chunk of debris, and tries to break the window with her hand. She fails; the glass is shatterproof. She sees her bloody handprint on the glass.

A woman's voice calls out, "Is anybody there?"

"I'm here!" Moody answers.

"Who is it?" the voice says.

"It's Sheila."

"Sheila, my skin is burning. I feel like I'm on fire."

The smoke thins for a moment. Moody can make out the woman's silhouette—it's Antoinette Sherman, a budget analyst she'd met earlier in the morning. Moody had complimented Sherman then on her purple sweater.

Now the color of Sherman's sweater is unrecognizable. It looks as if it's melted onto her body.

Sherman begins to pray aloud.

Am I going to die here? Moody thinks. "Jesus, help me!" she cries. "I don't believe You brought me here to die like this."

9:43 a.m.
West Lawn, the Pentagon

Chris Braman sees an ambulance and fire truck pulling up onto the lawn. He runs toward the ambulance. From the corner of his eye, he sees flames rising and smoke billowing out of a huge crater on the west side of the Pentagon. The gaping hole extends almost the full five stories to the roof. He can feel the heat from fifty yards away.

Braman reaches a medical technician pulling equipment out of the vehicle. "I need help! I need help!" he shouts. "I have a lady and a baby!"

The technician turns; his eyes widen. Behind Braman, three men are carrying a woman who's burned from the back of her head to the back of her thighs. Her clothes have melted away. Her back has been fried into a bright pink, fleshy goo.

The three men hand the woman over to the ambulance crew, then turn and run back toward the impact point. Braman joins them. They are like a handful of salmon swimming upstream against a tide of thousands streaming out of the Pentagon.

On the way, Braman runs into Lt. Col. Ted Anderson, a congressional liaison. "I got my general out," Anderson says. He looks dazed.

"C'mon," Braman says. Together, they race toward the flaming building.

As they approach, Braman observes a curious sight—the shadow of a man in a second-floor window. The man stands absolutely still, and appears to be holding a cup of coffee. Only later does Braman learn it's the image of a victim burned onto the glass from the inside.

Just outside the Pentagon's outer wall, Braman and Anderson pause. *Dear Lord,* Braman prays, *give us strength for what we're about to do.* Reaching underneath his army staff polo shirt, Braman rips off part of his T-shirt, ties it around his face, and steps through the five-story hole in the Pentagon exterior.

It's dark and extremely hot—Braman's forehead feels instantly sunburned. His nose and throat burn as if he's swallowed hot chlorine. From somewhere far ahead come agonized groans and screams. The sensation is familiar; it's as if Braman has once again dropped into a combat zone.

The Ranger plunges deeper into the smoke. He finds a badly burned woman wearing what's left of a sweater. Moving quickly, he guides the woman to the safety of the Pentagon grass.

Braman turns to go back inside.

9:52 a.m.
Office 1E-472, the Pentagon

The instant after her prayer, Sheila Moody hears the hissing of a fire extinguisher. The sound is followed by a distant voice: "Is there anybody in here?"

"Yes!" she yells as loud as she can. "We're here! We're here!"

"I can't see you!" the voice says.

"I can't see you either!" Moody replies. "But we're here!"

The smoke and fumes intensify. Moody begins coughing. She has to bend over; she can barely breathe. The coughing gets worse. She can't shout to guide her rescuer. But a voice inside her head whispers instructions: *Clap your hands.*

Still bent forward, Moody starts clapping.

A moment later, Moody looks up and sees movement through the smoke. She can still hear the fire extinguisher; the flames between her and her rescuers are lessening. Seconds later, she gathers her strength, steps over debris, and thrusts her arm into a black cloud.

A hand on the other side grabs hold and pulls her through.

9:54 a.m.
Inside E Wing, the Pentagon

Chris Braman has been following the sound of the clapping. When he sees a hand extending from the smoke in front of him, he grabs it.

The woman's hair is singed, and she's bleeding from the nose. She has serious burns on her hands, face, arms, and back. But she can still walk. Braman hurries her through the flames, smoke, and debris as quickly as possible. The fireman with the extinguisher and a policeman who was also inside join them. On the grass about a hundred feet from the crash site, Braman hands the woman over to another man who will guide her to safety.

Braman turns and takes two steps back toward the impact point. He hears explosions coming from each side of the crater; shrapnel is flying everywhere. Propane canisters are disintegrating. They sound like fragment grenades and are just as dangerous.

People are yelling, "Get back! Get back!"

Suddenly, the roof and what remains of the floors around the crash site implode in a terrifying roar, sending up a plume of ash and smoke. The spot Braman pulled the woman from three minutes earlier is now buried under tons of rubble.

9:56 a.m.
West Lawn, the Pentagon

"Sheila! Sheila!"

Bewildered and standing on the grass, Sheila Moody looks in the direction of the voice calling her name. It's Louise Kurtz, sitting in a police car. Kurtz was at the copy machine at the moment of the crash. The blast blew out the window facing the parking lot. Despite third-degree burns over 80 percent of her body, Kurtz was able to climb through the window and escape.

For a few minutes, the women simply huddle together, comforted by the other's presence. Both are in shock. As more and more rescue personnel arrive on the scene, some set up a triage area. They're looking for the victims who are in the worst shape.

One technician stops to briefly examine Moody and Kurtz, then appears ready to move on. "No, no," Kurtz says. "I'm hurt. You need to take me now." The technician looks closer, agrees, and helps lay her onto a gurney and into an ambulance.

Now alone, Moody walks nearer to the triage area, sits down next to a guardrail, lowers her head, and raises her arms in the air in an effort to lessen the pain. She's still having trouble breathing.

"Jesus," she says, over and over. Right now it's the only prayer she can manage. "Jesus."

7:25 p.m.
West Lawn, the Pentagon

Chris Braman sits down on the grass next to a stack of litters. He's spent the last nine-and-a-half hours organizing rescue teams and trying to get back into the Pentagon, without success. First he was ordered away because of reports of another imminent terrorist strike. Later, fresh rescue personnel arrived to lead the hunt for survivors.

Other than a brief phone call to Samaria, Braman has been totally focused on the task at hand. He's had nothing to eat since his half-consumed bowl of raisin bran. He hasn't allowed himself to absorb what's happened. He doesn't know that all sixty-four passengers on American Airlines Flight 77 are dead, along with 125 victims at the Pentagon. He hasn't yet learned that this was part of a terrorist plot that killed thousands more at the World Trade Center and at the crash site of United Airlines Flight 93 near Shanksville, Pennsylvania. Braman has simply done what he can. He's relied on adrenaline and a body in peak physical condition to allow him to perform.

Now, however, that body is finally rebelling. Braman feels a wave of exhaustion pass over him. His face and arms are burned. His clothes are in tatters. He needs fuel and rest.

With people running crisscross patterns in front of him and the Pentagon still burning against the night sky behind him, he closes his eyes and passes out.

8:30 p.m.
The White House, Washington, D.C.

In a somber voice, President George W. Bush, speaking on live television, addresses the world: "Today, our nation saw evil, the very worst of human nature. And we responded with the best of America—with the daring of our rescue workers, with the caring for strangers and neighbors who came to give blood and help in any way they could....

"Tonight, I ask for your prayers for all those who grieve, for the children whose worlds have been shattered, for all whose sense of safety and security has been threatened. And I pray they will be comforted by a power greater than any of us, spoken through the ages in Psalm 23: 'Even though I walk through the valley of the shadow of death, I fear no evil, for you are with me.'"

Thursday

A Jeep Wrangler eases into a driveway in an Alexandria, Virginia, suburb. It's seven o'clock on Thursday night. Behind the wheel, Chris Braman is beyond exhaustion. He realizes he doesn't even remember the drive home.

For the last two days, Braman has been operating on autopilot. He woke up Tuesday night on the Pentagon lawn and went back to assisting recovery teams. While others put in shifts and then left to recover, Braman and a civilian named Eric Jones never left the site. There were no more survivors, but Braman helped bring out sixty-three bodies from the still-burning rubble. Finally, late Thursday afternoon, the head of the search team declared the area too unstable to continue work and ordered everyone home.

Braman stumbles out of the Jeep to his front door. He's outfitted in clothes two sizes too small, donated by the Red Cross. What's left of the polo shirt and black pants he had worn since Tuesday—now covered with chemicals and human remains—are stuffed inside a black trash bag in his right hand.

Samaria meets him at the door. She squeezes him in the longest, tightest embrace he's ever known. No words are spoken. He can feel her fear melting into tears of relief.

That night, lying with Samaria in bed, Braman can't sleep. He still hasn't processed what's happened, hasn't allowed himself to experience even a trace of emotion. He stares at a corner of his bedroom, but he isn't seeing the room. He's watching a replay of the last few days. It's as if he never left.

There is the Department of Defense police officer escorting a survivor, a building contractor, away from the crash site. A partially severed eyeball hangs from the contractor's left eye socket.

There is, inside the bowels of the Pentagon, the ankle-deep water, the twisted steel and wiring, the dark passageways, a combination of burning jet fuel, asbestos, carbon monoxide, and human matter—an unforgettable, bitter taste.

There are the bodies and the pieces of bodies: an arm, a foot, a pile of ash and rib bones, a left hand with a wedding ring and pink nail polish still visible on its fingernails.

There is the flash of anger at the stupidity of racial prejudice. People may have different skin colors, but on the inside, hearts, lungs, and every other organ look exactly the same.

There are the chaplains standing in the pools of water near the Pentagon entryways, administering prayers and last rites to each victim as the body bags are carried out. Looking from inside the blast zone, the silhouette of each chaplain is framed by sunlight in a kind of halo.

There is the sudden swell of pride and defiance at the site of a pristine Marine Corps flag still standing in its base at the edge of a fourth-floor office, now cut in half. There are the tears in the eyes of the Marine Corps attorney, one of the few survivors from that office, when he is presented with that same flag.

And there is the little girl. She's about seven years old, with long, curly blond hair. She's holding hands with her mother. They're standing in the dark, crowded recovery area set up by the Red Cross for families waiting for word on a loved one. The mother is talking to a relief worker. Her face is searching, grim, just beginning to accept the unimaginable. But the girl has an innocent, almost playful expression underneath the blond curls. She's doesn't understand. Not yet.

In his bed, the hours pass, but Braman can't sleep. Finally, early Friday morning, he sits up. Samaria is instantly awake.

"I gotta go," he says. "I gotta go."

Samaria looks at her husband and says nothing.

A few minutes later, Braman is back in the Jeep, speeding through the darkness on I-395. The freeway is eerily deserted.

Braman is passing the Shirlington exit ramp near the Pentagon when the image of the little girl returns. He thinks of his three daughters. He thinks of Samaria. He thinks of how close they came to losing their husband and father. He thinks of the little girl holding her mother's hand, waiting for a daddy who won't be coming home.

Suddenly, finally, it all catches up to him. Braman can't see the road; tears cloud his vision. He pulls over to the freeway shoulder.

For the next thirty minutes, Braman sits in his Wrangler and weeps.

Saturday

Lying on her back, Sheila Moody tries to find a comfortable position as she's transferred by ambulance from Arlington Hospital in Virginia to Walter Reed Army Medical Center in Washington, D.C. Her husband, Vincent, follows in another vehicle.

Moody has third-degree burns on her hands and the back of her arms as well as less severe burns on her face, back, and feet. But she's alive. Of the thirty-four members of her office at the Pentagon, only she, Louise Kurtz, and their supervisor will survive. Antoinette Sherman will die in an area hospital in a few days. Moody will be the only one of the three survivors who recovers sufficiently to return to work.

On her way to Walter Reed, Moody knows how fortunate she is. On September 11, she was taken by ambulance to Arlington Hospital. A nurse tried and failed to contact her husband by phone that afternoon, but she was able to reach Moody's father in Maryland. Moody vividly remembers the one-sided conversation.

"Daddy, it's me. I'm okay," she said.

At the sound of his daughter voice, Moody's father burst into sobs.

"It's all right," she said. "I got hurt. I'm burned. But God protected me. I'm still alive."

Now, Moody stares at the ambulance ceiling. She isn't sure why God chose to preserve her out of all the people in her office, but she's sure that her survival isn't a coincidence. Somehow, her new job at the Pentagon, her decision to come in that morning, the location of her cubicle, and of course, the man who reached out his hand to pull her through the flames and smoke, are all part of His purpose.

Sheila Moody has a second chance at life. She decides she'd better make the most of it.

Sunday

Chris Braman is sitting in a pew at Calvary Road Baptist Church in Alexandria. Samaria is at his side. Braman is in a daze; he barely registers what the pastor is saying.

Gradually, it dawns on him that the pastor is talking about the terrorist attacks. They're showing slides of the Twin Towers and slides of victims and wreckage at the Pentagon. The scenes are horrifyingly familiar.

A sense of panic hits Braman. He's having trouble breathing. He feels trapped. *I have to get out of here!*

Braman jumps up, hurries to the back of the church, and runs outside. He crosses a sidewalk and falls to his knees beside a tree, trying to slow his breathing. As on September 11, his senses are on full alert—he can feel the breeze against his cheek; he can hear a leaf falling to the ground.

Footsteps slowly approach. It's Buzz, his Bible study teacher.

"Chris," he says. "I can't know or fathom what you're going through. But I'm here for you. Tell me what you need. I'm here."

The voice and words are calming. Braman's breathing gradually returns to a normal rate.

Braman and Buzz talk until the service ends, then return to the sanctuary. In the back of the church is a man in a wheelchair. Braman looks closer. It's his neighbor Rick, the man he'd threatened to kill a few months ago for taking a Taser gun to his dog.

Just a week earlier—two days before the September 11 attacks—Braman was shocked to suddenly realize why one of the men in his Bible study seemed vaguely familiar. *It's him!* Braman thought at the time. *It's Rick!*

Braman believed he hadn't seen his neighbor for months. But Rick had contracted a disease that vastly altered his appearance. He'd put on weight and was using a wheelchair.

When Braman realized this man was in his Bible study, he knew he had to say something—to apologize somehow for his earlier threats. The man may have done wrong, but Braman's response had only made the situation worse. Yet apologies weren't his usual style. What could he say that would make any difference?

Now, standing in the back of the church sanctuary, Braman suddenly feels as if he's waking up from a long, weary dream. All his life, he's been a proud warrior. He's fought for his family, his country, for a sense of justice in the world. He's followed his plan, trained hard, and served with distinction.

But has he served God?

Something, Braman realizes, happened to him during those terrible first hours after the attack on the Pentagon—not just to his body, but to his soul.

No matter how hard he trained, no matter how well he performed, things were going on here that were bigger than he could handle.

I've been humbled, he thinks. *I need God. We all do.*

Braman walks over to the man in the wheelchair and looks down at him. "Rick," he says, "please forgive me."

Rick reaches up to pull Braman down for an embrace. The man in the wheelchair begins to weep.

Monday

Chris Braman reports for work at the Pentagon on Monday morning and is ordered to get checked out at Walter Reed. He's also told to visit a patient there.

After his own exam, Braman finds the burn unit. For an hour, he sits in the hallway while the patient's bandages are changed.

Braman doesn't know why he's here. The patient's name is Sheila Moody, but he doesn't recognize it. He's just following orders.

Finally, he's allowed into the patient's room. The woman in the bed has bandages on her head, hands, neck, and back. Her arms glisten from a burn salve. A blue bandana is wrapped around the bandage on her head.

Yet Braman can see underneath the bandages that it's the woman he pulled out of the wreckage of the East Wing six days ago.

"Do you remember me?" he says.

The woman's eyes widen.

"It's you!" she cries. "It's you! It's you!"

Moody raises her arms, beckoning him closer. For the second time that week, Chris Braman receives a hug that communicates a thousand words.

Braman pulls up a chair and learns more about the woman he rescued. As they compare memories of the morning of September 11, he discovers that at the same moment he was praying for strength, Sheila Moody was asking Jesus for help.

"God sent you in there to bring me out," she says. "You're my guardian angel. I can't thank you enough for risking your life for me. It's a debt I can never repay."

Braman doesn't know what to say. He doesn't think of himself as a hero.

"You're here," he says finally. "That's my reward right there."

That evening, Braman climbs back into his Wrangler for the commute home. In some ways, so little has changed from a week ago. The interstate is again filled with bumper-to-bumper traffic. The billboards and exit ramps look exactly the same.

But Braman knows better. For him, after September 11, nothing will ever be the same.

But maybe that's not all bad, he thinks. He slides out of a slow lane and into a faster one. He'll be home soon. He's going to give Samaria and each of his daughters a very long hug.

IN HIS HANDS

> Like clay in the hand of the potter, so are you
> in my hand, O house of Israel.
> JEREMIAH 18:6

When a common fisherman named Simon—later called Peter—put down his nets to follow an unusual man from Nazareth, he didn't know what he was getting into. Soon enough, however, he discovered that he was risking everything: career, friends, future, his very life. He stumbled often, sometimes badly. Yet he persisted in his faith, allowing the Nazarene to shape him into a bold leader and the steady foundation of the early church.

It's the same for each of us. We accept the Lord's call but don't have a clear concept of what we're committing to. Soon we learn just how much He really asks of us. He seeks the death of our old selves. On the journey to that death, we frequently look for a way out and choose wrong paths. Yet if we continue to trust and persevere, offering ourselves as clay to the Master Potter, He will mold us into stronger, more beautiful, and more useful people than we could have ever become on our own.

Chris Braman has walked that trail. Though far from perfect, he is a man of faith who's put his trust and life in God's hands. In a

> *We must die to one life before we can enter another.*
> Anatole France

moment of crisis, the Lord used that trust to reshape him. His physical condition, a source of so much pride before, has deteriorated. Because of the chemicals he inhaled on 9/11 and the days that followed, he's pursuing medical retirement from the army and can't take more than a few steps without breathing difficulties. Yet Braman has no regrets. His faith and influence for the kingdom are greater than ever. He accepts invitations to speak around the country about 9/11 and God's role in that event and his life. Today he is more than a soldier for America—he's a warrior for the Lord.

"Absolutely, I've changed since 9/11," Braman says. "I'm walking in faith and not worrying about tomorrow. I don't argue with my wife so much. Petty things don't matter. I'm leading a Bible study and get into conversations about God all the time when I travel. I'm not worried about the possibility that I've shortened my lifespan because of the chemicals. I'm just trying to live every day for God."

Sheila Moody understands. She feels she's been given a second chance at life. Though it was a challenge emotionally, she returned to work at the Pentagon just a few months after 9/11.

"I can't take this blessing of my life that God has given me and turn and run and hide with it," she says. "I have to stand here and show the world how blessed I am and how marvelous the Lord is. I am totally humbled that God chose to preserve my life. It's had a profound impact on me. My marriage is stronger. My husband and I have a better appreciation for each other, our lives, our children. I see that everything can be taken away in the blink of an eye. What matters is family and what you do as a child of God. I just praise and thank Him and try to share my story with as many people as I can."

—JL

> It is, the writer of Hebrews says, a fearful thing to fall into the hands of the living God. He's dangerous, not safe at all. And yet there is something far more fearful and dangerous than to fall into His hands: to not fall into His hands.
>
> Mark Buchanan

Hostage in Paradise

BY BRUCE OLSON WITH JAMES LUND

It is a good morning for travel in the equatorial jungles of northeastern Colombia. I am in a dugout canoe on the Rio de Oro—the "river of gold"—with fifteen Motilone Indians, natives of this region. The rainy season is upon us, but the temperature is already more than one hundred degrees. Slivers of sunrays break through the clouds, striking abundant green fronds along the riverbanks and sending tendrils of steam skyward. Exotic birds, monkeys, and katydids, hidden in the lush forest all around us, offer a tumultuous chorus. This is a place of enchantment. Some would even call it paradise.

Steering our canoe is Jorge Kaymiyokba, a Motilone leader who has become my close friend over the twenty-six years I've lived and worked as a missionary among his people. We are family, he and I. The Indians in the canoe are my brothers and sisters. To an outside observer, I would appear out of place. I am fair skinned, a lanky six foot three, dressed in khaki shirt, pants, and sandals; the Indians are brown, stocky, at least half a foot shorter, and wear nothing more than a loincloth or hand-woven canvas skirt. Yet despite our physical differences, I feel truly at home with the Motilones; I am exactly where I belong on planet Earth. I am content.

I have no inkling that in the midst of this paradise, a terrible danger awaits, intending to strip away the peace in my heart.

It is October 24, 1988. We are bound for Saphadana, one of the trading posts I have helped the Motilones establish. As we journey downstream, I feel an unexpected sense of foreboding. I scan the shoreline—nothing. Everyone else seems in good spirits, so I try to relax. After a quiet hour and a half, we approach the cooperative.

Suddenly, I see them. In a clearing a few yards from the unoccupied trading post stand two guerillas dressed in camouflage. They carry rifles and machine guns. They're watching us intently.

The four major guerilla organizations in Colombia have operated in the adjacent regions for almost a decade, battling against the government and gradually controlling more and more of the area surrounding traditional Motilone territory. Their original aim was to help the poor and downtrodden people of South America, but many of the revolutionaries have been corrupted by power and money. And their methods are unspeakably violent.

I avoid glancing in the guerillas' direction, hoping not to provoke them. We move toward shore until our canoe hits the beach. When Kaymiyokba jumps out to pull the canoe farther up onto the sand, I turn my back. Then I step onto the beach. Immediately, a deafening noise splits the air, and the sand in front of me bubbles and erupts like a cauldron filled with boiling water.

"Out of the canoe!" a guerilla shouts. The rest of the Indians disembark. Several of the men march toward the guerilla pair, obviously intending to attack them with their bare hands. But one of the revolutionaries fires another volley in our direction; the bullets slam into the motor and rip a gaping hole in the side of the canoe.

"Lie down with your faces to the ground!" the same guerilla orders.

Kaymiyokba continues to walk toward the guerillas. I can see that he is struggling to control his anger. "Let's discuss this," he says in Spanish. "Let's not start something we'll all regret—"

"There's nothing to discuss!" the guerilla shouts, spraying the beach with his weapon as punctuation. One of his bullets grazes Kaymiyokba's forehead. The Motilone stands his ground.

"Bruce Olson is taken captive by the UCELN National Liberation Army!" the guerilla shouts, motioning at me to step toward him. This rebel group, commonly known as the ELN, is the only one of the four national revolutionary organizations that has not agreed to a recent, informal truce with the Colombian government.

I assess our situation, realizing I have only a few seconds to make a decision. There is no way we can successfully resist these men in physical combat; it's likely that there are more armed revolutionaries hiding nearby, and we have no weapons whatsoever, not even bows and arrows. I never carry arms, and on this trip I haven't even brought along a pocket knife—not that it would be any help against machine guns.

Are there other options? I could jump in the river and swim underwater to avoid the guerillas' bullets and possibly escape downstream. I know the area well, while the guerillas do not, so my chances would be good. But that would leave the Motilones at their mercy. I cannot risk it. And it would only put off this confrontation to another time, another place.

As the guerillas train their guns on me, I decide that the moment has come to face the enemy. But I will try to do it on my own terms.

I pick up the backpack I'd dropped when the gunfire started and tell Kaymiyokba in the Motilone language, "Don't follow me. Don't do anything!"

Then I speak to the guerillas: "I am Olson. I'm the one you want. Leave the Motilones alone."

I turn and begin to walk away from both the guerillas and the Indians. As I walk, about two dozen more guerillas emerge from the jungle. I ignore them and keep walking, hoping to put as much distance as I can between them and the Indians. Then someone shouts, "Stop! Stop or we'll shoot!"

I walk faster and shout over my shoulder, "You came to capture Olson. You can have me, but you'll have to come get me!"

A few guerillas start after me, walking as quickly as possible without actually running. Finally, when we are about five hundred yards from the Motilones, most of the guerillas abandon the Indians to chase me.

Suddenly, more revolutionaries appear in front of me. Using their weapons, they knock me to the ground and push my face into the wet earth. They kick me onto my back. One of them roughly shoves the barrel of a rifle into my mouth. I wince as metal scrapes against my teeth.

So this is how I'll die, I think. *From the bullet of a guerilla's gun.* I am surprised at how calm I am. But then I have done what I came to the jungle to do. If God has decided that my time for serving Him with the Motilones is over, who am I to question God? He will take care of them and complete the work He has started. I am at peace, and I will die without regret.

And so I wait for the explosion that will end my life.

To my surprise, the guerilla hovering over me with the rifle doesn't pull the trigger. Instead, he grabs my arm and yanks me to me feet. About thirty guerrillas close in. One ties my hands behind me.

The rifle jabs me in the back, pushing me toward the jungle. It is time to march. I catch a last glimpse of my friends on the beach, still covered by a pair of guerillas with machine guns. Kaymiyokba and the rest are watching closely but making no further moves to resist. *Good,* I think. *Perhaps they will escape safely.*

Then I lose sight of them as I stumble forward into darkness.

Over the next three days, on foot and later by canoe, we travel deeper and deeper into the jungle. Finally we reach a makeshift camp. I am told I am only being detained because the leader of the movement wants to speak to me and that I will soon be released. But it quickly becomes obvious that this is a lie. There will be no early release. The guerillas have been ordered to capture me and await further instructions.

The rains are relentless. A makeshift shelter is constructed over my hammock at the camp, but it offers virtually no protection from the elements. I am always soaking wet. Even with the sun out, it is so humid that my shoes and clothes never dry.

Despite the circumstances, I am able to keep my spirits up. I don't blame God for my predicament or expect Him to orchestrate a miraculous rescue. He is the one who called me to leave friends and family in Minnesota at age nineteen for this exotic place. He is the one who stirred a growing love in my heart for the indigenous tribal people of this continent. It was His quiet voice that told me I would never be happy, never have a moment's peace, until I obeyed His call.

Now it is still my responsibility to serve Him, right where I am. *Father,* I pray, *I'm alive, and I want to use this time constructively. How can I be useful to You today?* I know that He, not my captors, is in control.

I awoke to the fullness of His sovereignty many years before during a Motilone hunting expedition. Our intrusion into the jungle that day brought the usual reaction from assorted birds and monkeys, but as we quietly slipped through the dense undergrowth, I noticed a sudden escalation in the volume and intensity of the cacophony. Thousands of katydids joined the animal squawks and screeches, raising the noise level to the point where our human voices were drowned out. I'd never heard anything like it.

Astonished, I shouted to the Motilone ahead of me on the trail, "Listen to that! Isn't it incredible?"

He nodded. "Yes," he called back, "we heard it too. It's a piping turkey!"

His remark stopped me in my tracks. A piping turkey? All I'd heard was a chaotic, ear-shattering racket! How could anyone notice the voice of one lone turkey in the midst of this din?

My companion saw my confusion and signaled me to stop and listen. It was several minutes before I began to pick out which sounds were which—animals, birds, insects, humans. Then, slowly, the separate voices became more distinct. Finally, after more patient listening, I heard it. Behind the hue and cry of the jungle, behind the voices of my companions, behind the quiet sound of my own breathing was the haunting, reedy voice of the piping turkey, calling out as if it were inside a hollow tube.

It was a poignant moment for me. I wondered what else I'd missed—not only in the jungle, but also in my own spiritual life. How much had I overlooked when I'd failed to patiently tune in to God's subtle voice in the midst of life's chaos and stresses?

In the years that followed, the piping turkey often came to mind when I struggled to discern God's voice and sense His quiet presence during perplexing or discouraging situations. Over time, I developed the patience to see and hear God in the subscripts of life. And I learned from experience that even when I couldn't sense what He was doing, I could trust that He was always there, always working out His sovereign will, even when I was too overwhelmed by the "noise" to notice or appreciate His complex orchestrations.

As the days in the guerilla camp wear on, it becomes more and more important for me to remember that God has a purpose for my abduction. I have never had my freedom taken away from me. It is difficult to accept. But God has never let me down. I have to trust Him here—hidden in the jungle as a hostage of armed revolutionaries—just as before.

Or maybe more than ever.

One day, about a month after my abduction and after we have shifted between several camps, four guerillas approach me. They all wear camouflage; two carry rifles. I recognize one of the unarmed ones, a short man in his late twenties wearing a red beret, as the leader of the contingent that captured me.

I'd learned that his name was Alejandro. He directs one of the others to untie my hands.

Alejandro hands me a pad of paper and a pen. He speaks in crisp Spanish: "Olson, you will write letters to the chiefs of the Motilone Indians. Tell them that the ELN wishes to begin a peaceful dialogue with them. Tell them that you are well and that you believe it is wise for them to consider incorporating with us."

So here it is, finally. The guerillas want me to use my influence with the Motilones to manipulate them into an agreement: free passage and use of their territory in exchange for peace and, presumably, my release.

Without a word, I scribble out a statement in Barí, the Motilone language, explaining where I am in the jungle and the situation I am in and advising my friends to assess the area with great caution. I hand the note to Alejandro.

"This is no good," he says after looking at it. "We don't want you to write in the Indian language. You must write in Spanish." He hands me the pad again.

This time I write that I am alive and well as a political prisoner of the revolutionaries. The guerilla leader reads my message.

"This says nothing about beginning a dialogue. You must write more."

"No," I say. "I am happy to communicate with the Motilones, but I will not encourage them to begin a dialogue with the ELN or any of the guerilla movements. That is a decision only they can make."

Alejandro stares at me. A macaw screeches in the distance. One of the guerillas coughs.

"You must write this," Alejandro says, his eyes boring into mine. "If you do not...you will regret your position."

I shake my head.

Alejandro's face turns red. He speaks to an associate, who leaves for a few minutes, then returns carrying a chain about two meters long. Alejandro grabs the rifle held by one of the guerillas standing next to him. He points it at me, then at a barely discernable path at the edge of the camp.

"Walk," he says.

Our procession continues for a distance of perhaps two hundred meters. I can no longer see or hear any sign of the camp.

At Alejandro's direction, his associate fixes one end of the chain around the thick trunk of a palm tree and attaches the other end to my left leg.

The guerilla leader again stares into my eyes. "This will give you something to think about. We will return in two hours."

He turns on his heel and walks away, followed by the others. About ten meters away, the two armed guerillas stop and take up positions to watch me.

The two hours pass. Then the evening. And then the night and the next day and the day after that. Except for a change of shift of the guards every few hours and the daily delivery of one serving of yucca roots, I see no one. No one speaks to me. I am alone.

I am in for a long wait.

The days turn into weeks. I am wet and cold. My clothes begin to rot. The meager rations of roots take a toll on my health. I develop diverticulitis, a digestive disorder that causes abdominal pain, cramps, fevers, nausea, chills, and—when allowed to fester—internal hemorrhaging. My body is deteriorating.

Even so, I am not angry with God. I cannot judge Him. But I am disappointed in myself. Perhaps if I had been more intelligent or coy, the guerillas would not have captured me. Maybe I have not responded correctly to the responsibility He has given me.

Either way, I have the peace of His sovereignty. I have to remember that.

As I enter what I estimate to be the fourth month of my confinement to the palm tree, my situation grows more desperate. The diverticulitis intensifies. In addition to the headaches, chills, and stomach cramps, I begin to bleed internally. It appears that I am going to die here, shackled to a palm tree in the jungle. I am content if this is God's will. But I know it will be difficult for the Motilones. I long to be with them.

As I contemplate these things one evening, cold, hungry, and discouraged, I raise my head and spy a movement. There, about eight meters above me in the trees, is a Motilone Indian wearing a loincloth. I don't recognize him, but I am thrilled to see him.

There is something strange about his position. I squint my eyes, trying to get a better view. I realize that he isn't grasping the limbs of the trees. I don't understand how it is possible, but he appears to be suspended in space.

The Motilone hums and whistles to me in Barí. Because the Motilones employ a tonal language, communicating through a combination of high, mid, and low tones, I understand what he is saying. No words are articulated for the guards to hear.

"The tribal elders have asked me to find you," he says.

"Be careful," I whistle back. "The guards will see you. They have fire sticks." But the guards don't seem to notice. The Motilone is well camouflaged behind branches and leaves.

"If you release me from the tree, then encircle the camp and shoot some arrows, I may be able to escape," I whistle.

"No," he responds. "That is not why I am here. I have come to stop the disease inside you. I come to give you warmth."

Immediately, I feel a change within my body. The cramps subside. I *am* warmer. And I sense that somehow the internal bleeding has ceased as well.

"You will be released," the Motilone whistles. "But not yet. It will be soon, at the proper time."

I am overwhelmed. Something inexplicable, supernatural, is happening. I put my head down, which is the Motilone way of honoring the person before you. When I bring my head back up, the Motilone in the trees is gone.

Growing up, I never understood angels. To me, they were something carved in a stone altar or depicted in Renaissance art, nothing more. I read about them in the Bible but could never quite bring myself to believe in them.

When I was translating the New Testament into Barí, I attempted to explain the concept of angels to the Motilones. "But I really do not understand angels," I said. "I don't know how to translate this into your language."

They grinned. "We know what you are trying to say to us," one said. "You're speaking of a *ChigBarí*—a messenger sent by God. It can have a physical body or be a spirit." The Motilones understood angels better than I did.

The Motilone in the trees, I am sure, was a ChigBarí. And I am overjoyed that God has answered the prayers of my friends through this messenger of healing and hope. No matter how desperate and alone I feel, God is with me. He still loves me. I can still entrust my life to Him.

The next day, after four months of misery and isolation, the guerillas unshackle me from the tree and bring me back into their camp. The worst is over.

Or so I think.

I sit on the ground, my hands tied in front of me. I've been clothed in camouflage, the same as the guerillas. Guerillas walk past without even glancing my way. Several carry weapons.

It is the spring of 1989, a few days after my release from the palm tree. I have observed about seventy revolutionaries in the camp. Most are in training for combat. A few are recovering from previous confrontations with government troops. They are treated by ELN physicians and nurses under palm-thatched canopies hidden beneath the trees. I do not know what the guerillas have planned for me now. I'm not sure that they know either.

With nothing else to do, I pick up a stick and trace, as well as I can with my hands bound, the letter *A* in the dirt. *A* is the most significant letter in the Barí language. It stands for speech and life. Every Motilone name ends with this vowel. It means he or she possesses life.

A pair of worn boots appears in front of me. I look up. It is a guerilla, probably in his early twenties, with a dark face and black, bushy eyebrows. He has a pistol tucked into his belt. He is examining my scratches in the dirt.

The guerilla crouches down, picks up another stick and, copying my work, traces his own *A*.

"Ah," I say.

"Ah," he repeats.

Now I write *"mamá"* in the dirt—Spanish for *mother.* Again, the guerilla traces the letters. So I write *"amo me"* in front of mamá—I love my mother. He copies this, too, and I explain what it means. His face softens and acquires a faraway look. Then he focuses back on me, his eyes shining with satisfaction.

I bask in the warmth of his expression. Here is a revolutionary who loots banks, shoots helicopters out of the sky, and sabotages oil pipelines—a man trained to kill—yet he is tender about his mother. He obviously cannot read or write, yet he has an interest in literacy, in learning. This is more than a cold, calculating enemy. I am dealing with a human being again.

Later, I am able to write other short phrases on paper that my new "friend" also copies. One of the camp *responsables,* as the guerillas call their officers, observes this interaction and asks if I would consider teaching literacy to more of the guerillas. So we start a simple school, an hour and a half each day. It is the beginning of a change in my relationship with my captors.

I become a camp cook, learning quickly that all of the cooking has to be done during the night when the smoke is undetectable. I show others how to produce an elixir effective in controlling diarrhea by grinding selected leaves. I help them produce a natural oil from tree bark that relieves asthma. Because I knew how to extract teeth with forceps, I become the camp dentist. I even write flowery love letters for the illiterate rebels to send to their sweethearts.

Meanwhile, the literacy classes are invigorating for the guerrillas and for me. They lead to a whole curriculum of study: reading and writing, ecology, history, geography, and social and political sciences. Many of the guerillas had received little or no schooling and are eager to prove themselves.

The *responsables* encourage my teaching. They see my interest as evidence that I am coming around to their way of thinking. Many of the officers attend classes as well. I am careful not to overtly inject my values into our discussions. I know that my time as instructor would end abruptly if I am too candid or forceful. Eventually, however, the guerillas ask about my motivations and why I don't hate them for depriving me of my liberty.

This is a clear opportunity to talk about my faith, but I resist their questions. Something tells me the time isn't right, and I've learned to obey these inner impulses, knowing that God gives them to me for a reason.

A couple of weeks later, I am allowed to have a Bible. It becomes very precious to me. Through my translation work, I have already committed much of the New Testament to memory—but to have God's Word in my hands again is an unbelievable blessing. Again and again I turn to the Psalms for strength and reassurance: "Because he loves me," says the LORD, "I will rescue him; I will protect him, for he acknowledges my name. He will call upon me, and I will answer him; I will be with him in trouble, I will deliver him and honor him" (Psalm 91:14–15).

Not long after—and only on Sundays, so as not to appear overly intrusive or evangelistic—I begin to answer the guerillas' questions about God and my personal faith. As I talk about what Christ means to me, I notice tears in the eyes of several guerillas. Despite their violent training, these are idealistic, even thoughtful, men. The love and compassion of Jesus mean something to them.

A few of these men accept Christ. These are profound moments, times when God's Spirit manifests Himself so beautifully, so tenderly, that hardened terrorists often break down and weep as they receive Him into their lives. For me, the most touching part is that it is not my concept of God they accept; it is the very real, very personal Jesus Christ who meets them within the context of their own experiences, culture, and understanding.

I feel privileged to witness these conversions. Incredibly, some of my captors have become my brothers.

I never tell these new Christians that they have to leave the guerilla movement, though they sometimes ask me if they should. Instead I tell them: "You belong to Jesus Christ now. You must answer to Him, not to me."

Soon I have evidence that Christ is indeed speaking to these young men. A Christian guerilla creeps to my hammock late at night and shakes me awake. "Papa Bruchko," he whispers, "I have heard that you may be executed." I am silent at this disturbing message. It is not good news, but it is hard to know what to believe anymore.

The young believer keeps whispering. "I want to tell you that if I am ordered to execute you, I have decided to refuse." This means, of course, that he himself will be executed for disobeying an order. "I am with you," he says, "even if it costs me my life."

I know this man, and I believe him. His words move me deeply. I feel the strong presence of Jesus that night and am comforted.

After that, I shuttle from camp to camp, continuing my classes with some of the same students while meeting many new ones. But this relatively tolerable time with the rebels is about to end. Soon the local *responsables* insist that I make a decision: join the movement or face execution.

I refuse to join. As a Christian, I cannot justify killing to attain social and political goals. I know that my refusal means a death sentence. I am not eager to die, but I will not turn my back on the teachings and compassion of Christ.

The guerillas next pressure me to sign a public "confession" of my crimes against humanity. I refuse. "I've done nothing," I say. "You are asking me to lie. I have to tell the truth."

"Then we will kill you," I am told.

"The truth," I answer, "is a good thing to die for."

The guerillas try to break me, using an assortment of ploys. They begin with psychology. "The Indians have totally abandoned you," they tell me repeatedly. "Your programs are in disarray. We've talked to them, and not a single one cares whether you live or die. You might as well save yourself because no one else will."

Then comes the "good cop/bad cop" approach. Some guerillas are especially kind and friendly to me. Others are crude and cruel. Both try unsuccessfully to coerce me into championing their cause or influencing the Indians toward them.

Finally, I am turned over to the guerillas I call thugs. I am to be punished for my lack of cooperation. Their instruments are huge dowels made from the trunks of trees. These must weigh close to one hundred pounds each. I am made to lie down, and the dowels are rolled repeatedly over my body, three or four times a day. I can feel my insides being crushed. They fracture my ribs and cause me to urinate and vomit blood. Even years later, I can barely write about these terrible memories.

After the dowels, I can hardly walk or breathe. Once, I am forced to march three hours to another camp where a man who gives massages is sent to me. When he sees the bruises all over my body, a look of shame comes over his face. "This is not revolution," he whispers to me. "We shouldn't be hurting and torturing people. But I am not a commanding officer."

Later, I suffer excruciating pain and eventually lose consciousness. When I awake, a masked physician is examining me. He discovers that I am bleeding internally again. He says that I have lost so much blood that I need a transfusion immediately or I will die.

I do not want the transfusion. I am ready to die. But I am not given a choice.

As I lie in a hammock, I hear an argument break out among the guerillas. They are fighting over who will have the honor of giving his blood to "Papa Bruchko," as they have taken to calling me. Finally a young guerilla, Camillo, wins the argument. His blood is A positive, like mine.

It takes a long time for the transfusion. First they put a needle in Camillo's arm. This soldier of the revolution, who has fought many battles, cringes when the needle is inserted. *Good,* I think to myself. *I hope it hurts a lot.* His blood flows through a filter and then is transferred into a tube that runs into my arm.

At one point our eyes meet. In the past, I saw Camillo hanging around as I led classes for the guerillas, but we did not speak. Now, I try to read his expression. There is an intensity there I do not understand.

I must have fallen asleep, because I awake in the middle of the night, alone and in pain. I try to separate myself from it, but I cannot. I feel empty and hollow. The intensity of my physical pain only increases the sadness I feel for everything I've experienced in the past few months.

Then the strangest thing happens: an Andean mockingbird known as a *mirla* begins to sing. The mirla never sings at night, yet this one's melody goes on and on. It is hauntingly beautiful and familiar somehow. The music is complex, set in a minor key. I strain to identify it.

Suddenly I understand—it is a tonal Motilone chant! The mirla has heard the Motilones singing and is mimicking their tones. I listen closer. The meaning of the song is, "I walk on the trail of life experiences to the horizons. No evil spirit can threaten me or take me from the security I know in Jesus. I am suspended in Jesus through my expression of faith."

I wonder if I am hallucinating or if this is another angel sent by God. It doesn't matter. The music restores my spirit. Just a few hours before, I had wanted to die. Now I feel myself coming back to life. I spy the full moon, its light pouring down through the thick jungle vegetation. It seems as if it is shining just for me.

In the morning, the sun's first rays filter through the jungle canopy into the camp, casting everything in a greenish hue. I am wrapped in my hammock like an enchilada when I hear soft footsteps.

Suddenly the hammock parts and a face fills my vision. It is Camillo. His nose almost touches mine; I can smell his foul breath.

"Bruce Olson, do you know who I am?" he says in a loud voice.

"Yes," I say. "You are the valiant Camillo."

"Oh, but I am more than that," he says. "Twenty-four years ago, my father, Don Jorge, committed suicide. My mother was left a widow with many children, including me. You and the Motilones sent food from the cooperatives—rice, beans, tomato juice, macaroni, sugar, and even delicacies such as peach nectar and crackers—to my family for two years without ever asking for payment.

"Many years ago, you saved my life. Now I am repaying you. I gave you my blood and kept you alive. You have guerilla blood in your veins. You are one of us."

Then Camillo embraces me. It is the first expression of warm, physical human contact I've had since I was abducted. I melt like wax in a fire.

Who could have imagined all those years ago that a simple act of compassion from the heart would one day save my life? Only God could reconcile these two situations so beautifully. I feel His presence more closely than ever.

I have endured hunger, suffering, and pain at the hands of my captors. But I do not hate them. And it is not my role to judge them.

Camillo is right. Despite my refusals to align myself with their movement, I have indeed, in a way, become one of them. I now have guerilla blood flowing through me and have experienced the warmth of their embrace. Though we usually fail to recognize it, we are all somehow linked in a common struggle to find solutions to our mutual problems: me, Camillo, the Motilones and other indigenous tribes, the guerillas, the entire citizenry of Colombia. It is a difficult concept to accept—and at the same time, a great comfort.

It is July 1989. I have been escorted to a meeting with the *responsable* with the red beret—Alejandro. It is a short visit.

"Bruce Olson, our patience with you has ended," he says. "You have refused to assist us in establishing a dialogue with the Motilone Indians, you have refused to accept your responsibility as a member of our movement, and you have refused to admit to your crimes against the people. You will be executed. You have three days to prepare yourself."

I stiffen. After months in captivity, the end has suddenly arrived.

"There is nothing special that I need to do," I say. "I'm ready. Why don't you just get it over with?"

Alejandro waves his hand at me as if swatting away a bug. "Three days," he says and orders me taken away.

I spend what are to be my last hours on earth doing exactly what I've done in the previous weeks—teaching, cooking, going about daily life as usual. If it is God's will for me to die, I can accept death. After my ordeal as a hostage, execution sounds more like a relief than a sentence.

The guerillas watch me closely during those three days. I wonder what they are thinking. By this time, more than half the guerillas in the camp have given their lives to Jesus. The *responsables,* I think, will have a hard time finding someone to shoot me. Even many of those who aren't Christians have become my friends. I worry about them, as I worry about the Motilones. But I know that God will complete the work He has begun in all their lives. My mission is over.

The morning of my execution is like any July day in the jungle. Pockets of steam rise into the air from places where the sun has broken through the canopy and struck the damp ground. I take a deep breath, relishing for one last time the fragrance of the jungle leaves.

It seems like any other day, except that no one speaks to me. Perhaps they do not know what to say.

I spend a few minutes reading psalms in my Bible. One of them is Psalm 100: "Enter his gates with thanksgiving and his courts with praise; give thanks to him and praise his name. For the LORD is good and his love endures forever; his faithfulness continues through all generations" (verses 4–5).

I thank God for enhancing my life by placing me in South America and joining me with the Motilones. I thank Him for providing relationships and warmth of family—including the guerillas who have become like brothers to me. I thank Him that even here, among those who torture and kill to achieve their purposes, I have shared life and felt His strong, peace-giving presence.

At midmorning, there is a stirring in the camp. Alejandro and two of his associates walk briskly in my direction. I am ordered to accompany them to a small clearing, where I am tied to a tree.

One of the *responsables* begins reading the charges against me, the same ridiculous statements I've heard before, while Alejandro and the others leave to round up the firing squad. The *responsable* in front of me declares that I have been sentenced to death by the "people's court." Then he steps forward with a blindfold.

"No," I say, shaking my head. "No blindfold." I want to look my executioners in the eyes.

Over the guerilla's shoulder, I see that Alejandro has returned with a group of guerillas carrying rifles. But there is a disturbance. One of them seems to be arguing with the *responsable*.

It is Camillo. I can hear some of the exchange. "Olson refuses to accept our social values," Alejandro says. "He will not accept responsibility to align the Indians with us."

"But it was my blood that kept him alive!" Camillo says.

"Yes," Alejandro says. "But we can no longer maintain him. And if he is released, he will become our enemy and bring in armed forces."

Camillo loses the argument. He and nine others with rifles—most of them new Christians—are ordered to stand in a line about ten yards in front of me. Slowly they shuffle into formation, Camillo somewhere in the middle. Many have their heads down.

These men are my brothers in Christ, and now they will shoot me. It is shocking to me to realize that they are about to raise their arms to execute me, but I try to understand their dilemma. In the code of the guerillas, there is no room for ambiguity. If they refuse their orders, they, too, will be executed.

Perhaps this way is better, I think. *If I am to be executed, it is best that it be done by a brother in the faith.*

One of the *responsables* goes down the line and hands out cartridges. There is a loud "click" as each slides into a rifle chamber.

Finally, the order comes to raise weapons. I brace myself, stand as straight as I can, and face the ten men before me. Several have tears in their eyes. One of these is Camillo. I focus on him last.

A *responsable* starts the count: "Five. Four.—"

O God, You are forever faithful!

"Three. Two.

Take me into Your arms!

One. Fire!"

My ears fill with the deafening sound of rifle reports. And I feel…nothing. The men in the firing squad stare at me. I stare back.

One of the men, a bewildered expression on his face, raises his rifle to examine it. Suddenly he exclaims, "They were blanks!"

In unison, the firing squad and I swivel our heads toward Alejandro. He is watching me intently. Our eyes meet. Almost imperceptibly, he nods. Then, without a word to me or his men, he turns and walks away.

It has been a cruel ruse, one last attempt to break me. They hoped I would change my mind, beg for my life, and choose to cooperate.

The ruse has failed. But after preparing myself emotionally and spiritually for death, I feel exhausted and disappointed. I thought I was going to heaven. Instead, I am still here, still a prisoner. Nothing has changed.

Camillo steps forward to untie me. With the others watching, he does not speak. But his eyes dance.

He helps me back to my hammock. "I was ready to die," I say quietly after lying down.

"I know," he whispers. "But God has His ways. I see that now more than ever. He must have another plan—for both of us."

He pulls me closer. "I never pulled the trigger," he whispers in my ear. Then he embraces me and walks away.

———

A few days later, another *responsable,* Federico, comes to me. "Bruce Olson, I have good news for you! You are being released. Are you happy?"

I am suspicious. I shrug my shoulders and say, "I'm indifferent. My concern is for the Motilone people, the solidarity of their traditional life and the protection of their territory, which is so vital to their future. What about them?"

"Yes, yes, we understand your commitment," Federico said. "We made an error when we kidnapped you. The charges against you have been dropped. It's an embarrassment to us that you've been held in our camps. If we've mistreated you, we hope you can find the grace to forgive us. We've decided to leave the Motilones as an autonomous people. You may continue your work among them as before."

I am incredulous. "Are there conditions to my release?"

"You are released without conditions," Federico says. "*Now* are you happy?"

"If this is true, I am indeed."

Federico's eyes actually fill with tears. Then he hugs me.

Two weeks later, after a long trek back to civilization through the jungles and rivers, I am finally released to a group of journalists on the Colombia-Venezuela border. It is July 19, 1989, almost nine months after my abduction.

I am free.

I immediately make my way through the jungle to rejoin the Motilones. When I arrive, the people and the children run to the trail to greet me, but the scene is not immediately euphoric as one might imagine. They simply draw near to me in a respectful manner, waiting for me to make the first gesture. I hesitate for a moment while I gain control of my emotions. Then I go over and touch them on the shoulders and stomachs—a Motilone sign of affection. They break out into shouts of jubilation. It is a joyous reunion.

I am back with my friends, my family, and this fills me with a wonderful sense of relief and contentment. I am home again. *But perhaps,* I muse, marveling at how I've survived the past few months, *I never left.*

I pick up one of the laughing Motilone children and follow the others along the trail.

BE AT EASE

> The peace of God, which transcends all
> understanding, will guard your hearts and
> your minds in Christ Jesus.
>
> PHILIPPIANS 4:7

Like most of us, Bruce Olson had his troubles as a teenager. "Friends" who mocked him. Parents who didn't understand him. A temper that often seemed out of control.

And then there was the confusing matter of God and Jesus. The God that Bruce had learned about in church was a frightening deity of judgment and justice. But His Son seemed another story. According to what Bruce read in his Bible, Jesus was full of love and acceptance. Everyone who met Him found peace.

Bruce wanted that peace too. That's why, late one night in his bedroom, he prayed for Jesus to enter his life and deliver him from his fears. To his amazement, Bruce began to feel a change that very moment—a sense of peace coming into him, something alive, making *him* alive.

Bruce wasn't sure what he'd done. But he knew he never wanted that connection, that impression of being content and right with God, to go away.

> *Peace is not the absence of conflict; it's the absence of inner conflict.*
>
> Unknown

Many of us, when we give our hearts to Christ, discover that joyful sense of peace, the deep satisfaction that comes from knowing we belong to Him. The problem, however, is that over time we often lose that sense of belonging. We know God is still out there, as glorious and inspiring as a pristine, tropical jungle or the highest, snowcapped peak. But we can't seem to find Him; the clouds have rolled in, obscuring our vision.

It may be that we've allowed the fog to hide the meaning of God's peace.

In *Your God Is Too Safe,* author and pastor Mark Buchanan wrote, "We've made God too safe. I mean that we want Him to be comfortable rather than comforting. I mean that we want Him to be peaceable, to keep His peace, to be docile, rather than to be peacemaking and peace giving. And instead of being our hiding place, we would prefer that God be our ace in the hole."

Do you ever view God this way? Do you want Him to be peaceable instead of peace giving? Do you prefer Him as a member of the local search-and-rescue squad, standing by with a chopper and rope and a team of dogs, just in case?

God isn't like that. He's not a waiter lurking in the shadows, ready to refill our water glasses or present a new supply of bread when we give the signal. He's the Master of the universe. He's calling *us* to move up the mountain, step into the clouds, and find Him. The call may be to take the initiative and start praying daily with your spouse. Or to quit your job for that ministry opening in another state. Or to just get off the couch and help your neighbor carry in her groceries. Only you, through prayer, Scripture reading, and the advice of trusted friends, can discover the unique plans the Lord has in mind for you. But make no mistake—once you understand the route, He fully expects you to strap on your crampons and set out for the next camp.

Bruce Olson figured it out. He realized as a teenager that the peace in his heart would be fleeting unless he answered God's call. Though he loved languages and dreamed of becoming a linguistics professor, Bruce's heart was stirred after he attended a missions conference. He found himself drawn more and more to the people and

culture of Colombia and Venezuela, in particular a tribe of native
Indians called the Motilones. He thought and prayed about it.
Crazy as it seemed, he realized that God was calling Him to deliver
the good news to a primitive, often violent people in a remote jungle in South America.

It wasn't easy. It certainly wasn't safe. Yet through his faith and
risky obedience, Bruce Olson experienced God's active, powerful
peace—a peace so strong that even war-hardened revolutionaries
could not strip it away. In fact, it was in the hardest places that
Bruce was most calm and content
and most effective for the kingdom.

Think about that for a moment.
You'd expect a man who'd been kidnapped, tortured, and threatened

> Live carefree before God;
> he is most careful with you.
> 1 Peter 5:7 (MSG)

with death to be a mess, right? Wouldn't we all be in that situation?
Of course—unless we chose to rely on a greater power and realized
we were right where He wanted us.

Solomon, writing as the personification of wisdom, says in
Scripture: "Whoever listens to me will live in safety and be at ease,
without fear of harm" (Proverbs 1:33). Through the old king, I
believe God is giving us a message.

Read that passage again. God says *listen,* but He doesn't mean
hear the words and ignore them. He wants us to act. He wants us to
obey. He says that if we do, we'll *live in safety.* I don't think He's
talking about physical safety here. Obeying His call will sometimes
take us to the most dangerous places—maybe even in front of a firing squad. Yet even there, even if we die for our obedience, our soul
will be safe for eternity. And that's a comforting, peace-giving
thought.

If we listen and obey, we'll also *be at ease.* We'll know God's
peace in our moment of greatest stress. Imagine what you dread

most—say, jumping out of an airplane at ten thousand feet, stumbling into a pit filled with crocodiles, or teaching your daughter how to drive. Then imagine being in that moment, flooded with an overwhelming sense of God's presence and peace. You're thinking, *I can handle this, no problem. God's got it under control.* You're *at ease.* Wouldn't that be a great way to go through life?

Finally, God says that if we follow Him, we'll operate *without fear of harm.* He's talking about our attitude here. He's promising that we'll be fearless. Courageous. Daring. Free to boldly go wherever He sends us. I want more of that! How about you?

Bruce Olson has lived his life this way, listening and obeying, courageous in the face of death, safe and at ease in the arms of his Father. You may not be Bruce Olson. But God still has His hand out. He's offering His peace to you as well. Will you step into the clouds to find it?

—JL

The Last Lagoon

BY JAMES LUND

Ted Roberts mentally taps his foot as he waits for Jack, the dive master. Roberts is outfitted in full scuba gear: blue wet suit, face mask, air tank, regulator, camera, flashlight, and swim fins. He's standing on a black mat at the stern of the 132-foot-long *Odyssey,* a sleek former cruise ship that now serves as a dive vessel. The setting this morning is idyllic: sunlight shimmers off waters that sparkle in every shade of blue and green; palm trees sway gently on a distant island. But Roberts isn't here to admire the view. He wants to be in the water.

Roberts is beginning the fourth day of a diving vacation in Chuuk (rhymes with Luke) Lagoon, home of a group of seven islands in the South Pacific, three thousand miles southwest of Hawaii. Formerly known as Truk, Chuuk is part of history and is considered one of the world's premier wreck-diving destinations. Most of the twenty-odd divers and crew aboard *Odyssey* have friends to plumb the depths with, but Roberts is here alone, so he'll wait for the dive master. No one is allowed to dive solo.

Jack finally emerges from the bowels of the dive ship and steps onto the platform. They've already held a briefing this morning; words aren't needed now. Jack takes a long stride off the platform and quickly disappears beneath the aqua surface. Roberts tugs at his face mask a final time, inhales deeply, and plunges in after him.

It's August 2005, the rainy season in Chuuk, but the water is a tropical eighty-two degrees. Roberts is surrounded by an explosion of bubbles, but after a few moments he picks out the dive master below and slowly follows. He's pinching his nose as he descends, allowing his ears to equalize to the pressure. As he drops deeper, the colors from the surface fade away and are replaced by an inky dark blue. The only sound is his rhythmic breathing through the regulator.

For Roberts, a fifty-nine-year-old bundle of hard-driving energy, scuba diving is part adventure and part escape. He loves his job as senior pastor of a large church in Gresham, Oregon, but also feels the pressure that comes with it. Here, submerged in a lagoon in the South Pacific, there are no questions, no responsibilities. It's just him and the ghosts of another era.

At thirty feet below, a vessel suddenly appears. Constructed in 1939, the *Shinkoku Maru* was once a heavily armed oil tanker and member of the proud Japanese fleet. She was one of eight oilers that refueled her nation's warships during the devastating attack on Pearl Harbor in 1941. She also participated in the Imperial Japanese Navy attack on the island nation of Ceylon (now Sri Lanka) in 1942.

The *Shinkoku Maru*'s history of success was short lived, however. The Japanese had considered Chuuk Lagoon an ideal hiding place for its fleet. The lagoon was protected by fifteen islands and a circular, one-hundred-forty-mile barrier reef. Concern about Allied advances led Japan to relocate its aircraft carriers, battleships, and heavy cruisers in early February 1944. But the *Shinkoku Maru,* along with many other small warships and merchant ships, stayed behind. When a major Allied attack on Chuuk, dubbed Operation Hailstone, began on February 17, the remaining Japanese fleet was nearly helpless. After two days of relentless attacks and a pair of aerial torpedo hits, the *Maru* went down.

Roberts considers all this as he examines the *Maru*'s bridge, which is blanketed in coral that reflects a rainbow of colors from the beam of his flashlight. He has tasted battle himself. As a U.S. fighter pilot during the Vietnam War, he flew on nightmare-inducing missions that took the lives of many of his friends. What horrors did the men on the *Shinkoku Maru* face in their final moments? How many loved ones did they leave behind? The Japanese were certainly the enemy at the time, but Roberts feels a comradeship with the souls lost here, a kinship with fellow warriors and sufferers.

The 500-foot-long *Shinkoku Maru* did not sink upright all those years ago; it sank on its side on a stretch of lagoon floor that lies at a steep angle. The *Maru*'s bow is forty feet below the surface, while the stern is nearly 130 feet into the depths. Roberts, accompanied by Jack, examines the ship's bow gun. It is covered with coral. A rubber gas mask rests at the foot of the gun.

Moving aft, Roberts plays the beam of his light over the deck. The area is teeming with marine life; schools of batfish circle endlessly, and the coral-carpeted deck is filled with tiny shrimp, crabs, and worms. Still visible underneath this idyllic layer of life, however, are Japanese shells and other instruments of war. Roberts keeps swimming, past the bridge, a large mast, and a smokestack, to the point where the *Maru* received its fatal blow: the engine room. Here, he sees a hole large enough to drive a jeep through. When the torpedo struck, it ruptured an empty fuel tank and detonated the fumes, creating the explosion that sealed the fate of the *Maru* and its crew.

Roberts stops to snap a photo. *It sure would be fascinating to go in and see what's there.* But he knows his time on this dive is already nearly up. And penetrating the hull of a sunken vessel, especially one this size, is dangerous business.

There are so many ways for the shipwreck diver to die. With visibility minimal at best, an inadvertent cut of an air hose by an unseen broken pipe or the surprise appearance of a tangle of cables can spell doom for even the most careful diver. And then there is nitrogen narcosis, every undersea explorer's nightmare. At depths greater than about sixty-six feet, a diver's judgment and motor skills begin to erode. At more than one hundred feet below, the impairment can be significant. Many a diver, confused by narcosis, has lost his way inside the twisting labyrinth that is the guts of a shipwreck. And the diver in trouble—say, extremely low on air—cannot simply shoot for the surface. He must rise gradually, allowing the nitrogen he's accumulated from his breathing gas to release into his bloodstream in tiny bubbles. If he surfaces too quickly, he risks the "bends"—large bubbles that form outside the bloodstream and block circulation. The result can be agonizing pain, paralysis, and death.

Deep-sea divers learn techniques, including laying down line, that help them minimize the dangers of narcosis. But though Roberts has been scuba diving for years, he's never taken those courses. He isn't certified for going inside a wreck.

Thirty minutes later, Roberts is back on board the *Odyssey*, removing his gear and rinsing off. One of the crew's dive masters approaches. It's Kevin—blond, in his twenties, fit, and cocky. He sits at a table nearby.

"So," Kevin says, "you want a real exciting dive?"

Roberts picks up his camera. He wonders what Kevin means. "Yeah," he says, "that sounds interesting."

"It's about twenty minutes of pitch black." Kevin says. "Going through the inner workings, going below the machine shop, down on the third deck."

Roberts looks at Kevin, who's watching closely for his response. He feels a surge of testosterone kick in.

This young buck is challenging me, Roberts thinks. *He wants to see if I've still got my stuff. Am I going to let this go unanswered?* A faint voice from within is telling Roberts *No, don't do this,* but he pushes it aside.

"Sure, I'm in," Roberts says.

Kevin grins. "Good. I'll meet you down there on the next dive."

By eleven that morning, Roberts has hooked up with two other divers and is ready for his second effort of the day. He scans the stern of the *Odyssey*—no sign of Kevin. Roberts and his two partners jump in.

Now that he knows the layout, Roberts can make a closer inspection of the *Shinkoku Maru*'s hull. He's been down for about thirty minutes—half of his allotted hour—when the lights of two new divers appear. One of them, Roberts sees, is Kevin.

Kevin uses hand signals to communicate: Do you want to go inside?

Roberts checks his air pressure via the dive computer on his wrist. If he's going to allow himself twenty minutes or so to decompress before surfacing, he really doesn't have much time. But Kevin is waiting for an answer.

Again, Roberts senses an inner warning. For the second time, he ignores it. *Why not?* he thinks. *This is a once-in-a-lifetime experience. I'll just take a peek.* He flashes Kevin a thumbs-up.

Roberts waves good-bye to his two partners and joins Kevin and the other diver. Soon they are entering the oil tanker and descending to the machine shop: Kevin first, followed by Roberts, followed by the other diver. It is utterly dark here; with his light, Roberts can barely make out the blade end of Kevin's fin two feet ahead.

On the way through the machine shop, Roberts chances quick glances at the accoutrements of another time: a lathe, more tools, and an air compressor with broken gauges that look like eyes, creating the appearance of some sort of monster robot. Roberts wonders if the sailors working here had time to panic when the torpedo struck.

Kevin keeps swimming. They head down a narrow catwalk to another, deeper level. Roberts is twisting and turning to follow; the walls are bent at strange angles because of the long-ago explosion. Cable and wires dangle like spider webs, and pipes protrude from unexpected crevices. Here, where no sunlight can reach, the rainbow coral is absent. All is the color of rust. They are past one hundred feet now, a depth where the threat of narcosis is eminently real.

An alarm bell sounds in Roberts's mind: *My air supply!* His margin for escape is nearly gone.

Roberts has just completed that thought when it happens. Without warning, the diver behind Roberts blasts over and through him, knocking off Roberts's face mask and nearly kicking the regulator out of his mouth.

He's lost it! Roberts thinks. Sixty years worth of silt suddenly explodes in the narrow passageway, creating a brown snowstorm.

Roberts struggles to restore the position of his mask. When he does, he sees nothing but the swirling silt—no divers, no wreckage. Worse, when he tries to move, something behind him holds him in place.

He's trapped.

Terror wells up inside Roberts. He fights the urge to scream, to thrash against whatever is holding him. He remembers the first rule of deep-sea diving: if you panic, you die.

Roberts tries to slow his breathing—his air will be gone if he doesn't. He checks his air gauge: low—too low.

I'm going to drown down here. My wife is going to kill me! He sees no humor in the thought.

Roberts again tries to pull away from the thing behind him. He's stuck.

There's nothing like a crisis to trigger a searing self-examination. In the darkness, more than a hundred feet under water, questions suddenly rise to the surface of Roberts's brain: *Why do you put yourself in these situations? Why are you down here? What are you trying to prove?*

Unbidden, a memory flashes in his mind. Roberts is alone in his church office, preparing a sermon about the love of God the Father for His children. From nowhere, a voice speaks: *Ted, I want you to thank Me for your father.*

Roberts, sitting at his desk, is shocked. "You want me to what?"

I want you to thank Me for your father.

Roberts can accept that God is speaking to him. But he doesn't want to accept the words. Born an illegitimate child and raised by a single mother, Roberts endured six abusive stepfathers. His childhood was one long period of torment. Pain and abandonment were "normal." He longed to hear a father, just once, say, "Well done, son. I'm so proud of you." The idea of thanking God for his biological father goes against every fiber of his being. But Roberts is a military man, and years ago in a bunker in Vietnam, he gave God the authority to be his commanding officer. He's not about to stop obeying orders now.

Roberts stands, grips the back of his chair, and tries to find the words: "Dad, thanks for life. I never met you, and that grieves me. I think you would be proud of me. Hopefully I will meet you on the other side." The simple statement releases a torrent of pent-up grief. Roberts is wracked by long, hard sobs. As he weeps, however, he feels years of pain washing away.

In his prison deep inside the *Shinkoku Maru,* the memory unlocks a mystery for Roberts. He's been driven his whole life—even to the point of undertaking a dive he has no business making—to gain love or approval from others. He's been trying to make up for the love and approval he never received from a father.

It's a revelation to Roberts—but he wonders if he'll have the chance to make use of it. He reaches over his shoulder but can't stretch far enough to feel anything. He considers trying to slip off his oxygen tank so he can turn around, but knows it would be a time-consuming and potentially fatal maneuver. Without the weight of his tank, he could float away or become even more entangled.

I survived Vietnam, and I'm going to die here? he thinks. *This is nuts.*

Suddenly, a faint, opaque beam of light appears in the murkiness in front of Roberts. The beam grows stronger. It's Kevin.

The dive master has already pointed the "narced" diver to the surface. Now, coming back for Roberts, he sees he's stuck and reacts quickly. Kevin reaches over Roberts's shoulder and finds his air hose and buoyancy compensator wrapped around a catwalk. Working as fast as he can, Kevin unwraps the gear and frees Roberts. Alone, Roberts never would have had time to escape.

Roberts isn't in the clear yet; his air supply is nearly exhausted. He follows Kevin up through the darkness and back through the twisting passageway. He's trying to control his breathing, yet swimming as fast as he can, knowing every moment counts.

Soon—it can only have been a few minutes, but it feels like an eon to Roberts—they slip outside the hull of the *Maru*. They're free!

Seconds later, at a depth of about sixty feet, Roberts takes a breath on his regulator and realizes there's nothing there. His air is gone. He waves his arm rapidly at Kevin and points to his air hose.

Kevin understands. For the next forty feet, they "buddy breathe," taking turns on the dive master's regulator. At twenty feet, they reach a bottle of air hanging on a line from the *Odyssey* for just this kind of emergency. Once Kevin sees Roberts is okay and breathing with the new bottle, he surfaces, and Roberts is alone. For the first time since he entered the *Shinkoku Maru*, Roberts is able to let go of the tension inside. His emotions spill out.

You dingbat, he thinks. *You don't want to ever do that again. You have got to deal with this drivenness and your desire to prove yourself!*

The minutes pass as Roberts decompresses. He gradually becomes aware of how fortunate he is to still be breathing. He begins to see how his narrow escape from the innards of a shipwreck is a snapshot of his life. So many times, he's tried to power his way through situations, only to end up exhausted and defeated. His greatest successes were achieved only when he gave up control and listened to a more experienced—and eternal—voice.

The words of a favorite psalm come to mind:

God, make a fresh start in me,
    shape a Genesis week from the chaos of my life.
Don't throw me out with the trash,
    or fail to breathe holiness in me.

Bring me back from gray exile,
    and put a fresh wind in my sails!
Give me a job teaching rebels your ways
    so the lost can find their way home.
(Psalm 51:10–13, MSG)

God, you are so good, he thinks. *You were warning me the whole time not to go down there. Thank You for giving me a chance at a fresh start. Thank You for allowing me to find my way home.*

The current gently caresses Roberts as he hangs on to the line. He gazes up through the now light blue waters of Chuuk Lagoon to the surface, to the crimson orange glow from the world above, and to the life that still awaits.

NEVER DIVE ALONE

> I will instruct you and teach you in the way
> you should go.
>
> PSALM 32:8

There's a reason why wreck divers always swim in pairs: If one gets in trouble, the other is there to help him out of it. As Ted Roberts experienced firsthand, when exploring a shipwreck one hundred feet below the surface, the opportunities for "next dive" to become "last dive" are as abundant as the sea creatures that inhabit the deep.

Many of us have a knack for getting into trouble. Don't bother us with the details—we know what we want to accomplish, and we're ready to plunge in and seize the treasure waiting for us. For those born with an inclination to risk, this is second nature. And what, you may ask, is wrong with that? As we've already discussed, the list of benefits from risk is longer than the list of unexplored planets in our galaxy.

Yet there is a fine line between appropriate, godly risk and foolhardy action. Because the minute we begin taking risks based on our own intuition rather than on God's guidance, we're no longer bold and courageous explorers heading for a new frontier—we're just dumb chickens headed for disaster.

How high should the mountain climber ascend and how far should the arctic explorer travel if he has a wife and children at home? For that matter, is a missions trip to Africa always the right move? How many of us are risking in one area of life to avoid risk in another, such as developing a more intimate marriage, introducing a co-worker to Christ, or offering to spend time with a fatherless son in the neighborhood?

The answers to questions like these aren't always apparent.

That's why we must remember, whether we're diving inside a ship-wreck or standing on the precipice of a major decision, that we're not alone in making our choices. God is ready to whisper in our ears if we'll only ask and hear. "Listen, my son, and be wise, and keep your heart on the right path" (Proverbs 23:19).

> *You are as close to God as you choose to be.*
> Kenny Luck

Ted Roberts heard the whisper in Chuuk but chose to ignore it. That decision, he says now, was "massive stupidity. I should have died down there." Yet the Lord graciously used that mistake as a wake-up call for Ted, leading him to a new level of healing of past wounds and to a new direction in his ministry.

"God didn't design us to take foolish risks," Ted says. "He wants us to boldly risk for Him in faith. There's a world of difference. But even when we're giving in to our own foolish tendencies, He's still speaking to us, loud and clear."

—JL

Love and Loss in Iraq

BY CARRIE MCDONNALL WITH KRISTIN BILLERBECK,
RETOLD BY JAMES LUND

Carrie Taylor walks alone through the crowded, narrow streets of an Israeli-Arab village in northern Israel. She notices other women and children making furtive glances in her direction. Carrie is blond and American, which tends to attract attention in this part of the world.

After several minutes, Carrie reaches her destination: the post office. An Israeli soldier holding a rifle steps in front of her. "You can't go in there," he says.

"Why not?" Carrie asks.

"Bomb squad."

Carrie sighs. They don't take chances here. If an unidentified package or bag is left in town, a police team comes in and detonates it. Sometimes it's a sack of groceries, but once in a while, it's a bomb. The soldier points to the other side of town, indicating that Carrie must walk to the next post office.

She could be standing within five feet of a powerful explosive, but Carrie doesn't feel fear. The threat of violence is a part of life in the Middle East. She is a bit annoyed, though. It will take longer than she expected to return home.

In Israel, "home" for Carrie is one end of a converted metal shipping container. She is a missionary who works in a foster home for Arab children, where she cleans bathrooms, scrubs floors, and helps cook. The eight-by-eleven-foot "apartment" where she sleeps consists of tin walls with a hole cut out for a window, a toilet, and a shower. But Carrie has given the space her personal touch. A copy of the Mona Lisa hangs just outside her bathroom. Christmas lights adorn the ceiling. And pictures of family, friends, and favorite places—including the Sea of Galilee—cover the walls.

To a visitor, Carrie's life in Israel might appear a strange mix of threatening and mundane. It's not what most twenty-three-year-old, single American women would choose. Yet for Carrie, the opportunity has brought rewards that can't be measured. She has come to love the children in the foster home and the Muslim family that has graciously "adopted" her. She's developed a special affection for these people and their culture. She has fulfilled a calling and deepened her relationship with God.

Carrie has adjusted well, yet there are still occasional moments of loneliness. She sometimes wishes she could share her new life with someone.

At about the same time that Carrie begins her stay in Israel—the first months of 1999—a truck bounces along a deserted dirt road in Northern Sudan, raising a cloud of brown dust as it passes trees, bushes, and a few butte-like hills. Behind the wheel, David McDonnall keeps his eyes focused forward. He's looking for a remote village. There's no sign of human life anywhere, but David is unfazed. He's feeling "pretty dad-gum *kwayis*"—his version, in country-boy-Arabic-speak, of "pretty darned good." Nothing makes this twenty-five-year-old American missionary happier than the idea of introducing Christianity to those who have never heard the name *Jesus*. The mostly Muslim Sudanese definitely qualify.

Sudan is not the easiest place to serve. For most of the years since the nation established its independence in 1956, civil war has raged between Islamic-oriented government forces from the north and African groups made up of several religions in the south. The discovery of oil in the south in 1978 only intensified the bloodshed. But David, raised in the wilds of Colorado, with a big heart and an affinity for adventure, has sensed a call to this strife-laden region and these struggling people.

On this day, David and his co-worker, John, are on a trip to assess a village's need for food, water, and health care. John is in charge of the map. As far as they can tell, it's reliable—though in this part of the world, boundaries can shift almost daily.

Suddenly, on the side of the road about thirty yards ahead, four men armed with pistols and AK-47s step into view. "Stop the truck!" one yells in Arabic.

David must make a quick decision. He has no idea what group, if any, these men are affiliated with. They may be thieves.

He keeps driving.

"Stop! Stop!" the men shout again as the truck nears. David maintains his speed.

One of the men raises his AK-47 and sprays a round of bullets over the truck's hood. This time David hits the brakes.

With weapons aimed at David's head, the gunmen approach his window.

"Why didn't you stop?" says one holding a pistol.

"We thought you might be bandits," David replies in Arabic.

"Where are your papers?" the man says.

David and John pull out their identification papers and hand them over. They aren't what the man is looking for. Apparently, David and John have stumbled onto a restricted government road. They have no written permission to be here.

The man holding the papers waves his gun at David and John. "Out of the truck," he says. Not liking this situation but seeing few options, David, followed by John, complies.

The gunmen confer. David figures that if these men are indeed government soldiers, it's unlikely he and John will be shot. Still, David is uneasy.

The discussion ends. The pistol waver walks over to the missionaries. "You, stay here," he says, addressing John. "You," he says to David, "back in the truck."

David again sits behind the wheel. Another soldier with a pistol climbs into the backseat.

"Drive," the soldier says, pointing the gun at David.

David starts the truck and presses on the gas. *I don't know where this is leading,* he thinks. He begins to pray aloud in English.

"No talking!" the soldier says. "I don't understand what you're saying."

"I'm sorry," David says in Arabic. For the rest of the trip, he prays silently.

A few miles later, David and his captor arrive at an outpost manned by more government soldiers. David explains the situation—he is a relief worker whose map led him into an off-limits military area. This time, the officer in charge appears to believe him.

David is taken back to where he encountered the first group of soldiers. He's concerned about John. It turns out, however, that John has fared much better than David. In the best tradition of Arab hospitality, the soldiers have treated John to refreshments, then allowed him time alone to rest.

Despite what was a tense situation, David has to laugh. While he was riding around in the desert with a gun at his back, his partner was enjoying tea and cookies and taking a nap! It will make a good story for his co-workers.

———

Over the next several months, David McDonnall will accumulate material for a number of good stories. There is the time he sleeps through a major earthquake while on vacation in Turkey. Another time, he and his team are shot at in East Africa's Eritrea. There is also the run-in with police in Egypt and with a boy carrying a pistol in the Sudan. David's fellow missionaries dub him *Ya Sa'id Mushkalji*—Mr. Troublemaker.

David's next adventure, however, is a different kind of "trouble." On New Year's Day 2000, missionaries from throughout the region gather in the Israeli-occupied West Bank territory to celebrate the millennium. That night, David is introduced to a pretty, green-eyed missionary from Texas: Carrie Taylor. She too has an earnest desire to serve God and has developed a connection with the Arabic people, especially the children.

David is captivated.

What David doesn't know is that the night before their introduction, Carrie prayed to the Lord, telling Him about her hopes for a husband. She also wrote a letter to the then-anonymous man she hoped would one day become her life partner.

That evening on the West Bank, Carrie doesn't connect her prayer to David. In fact, she doesn't even get his name right—she calls him "Nathan." For Carrie, her first encounter with the outgoing missionary from Colorado is inconsequential.

Eight months later, again on the West Bank, Carrie and David meet for the second time at a Christian-sponsored basketball game. This night, after having more time to talk with him, Carrie is intrigued. She finds David warm and friendly, a wonderful storyteller, and funny.

A friend at the game pulls Carrie aside. "Have you known each other for a long time?" she asks.

"No," Carrie says. "We just met. Why do you ask?"

"Oh, I just noticed how comfortable you were with each other and thought you'd been friends for a long time. There seemed to be something more there."

Carrie is pleased that someone else notices the connection. She secretly hopes her friend is right.

Carrie returns to Israel, and David to his assignment in Jordan. However, their friendship thrives over the Internet in a Middle Eastern version of the movie *You've Got Mail.* They each share reports on their daily activities and their struggles in ministry and life.

As Carrie and David grow closer, conflicts drive other parties in the region further and further apart. By the end of 2000, a cycle of Palestinian attacks in Israel and retaliations by the Israeli army leave more than four thousand dead, mostly Palestinians. In October the USS *Cole* is attacked off the coast of Yemen, killing seventeen Americans. Everyone, including Carrie and David, learns to deal with daily tension.

Early in 2001 Carrie boots up her computer and sees an e-mail from David that creates a different kind of tension. The subject line is "honesty."

What is this about? Carrie thinks. *Is he going to tell me that we need to be honest with each other and he can't e-mail me anymore? Or is he going to share honestly what he feels about me?*

Carrie pauses, her finger poised over the computer mouse. *Regardless of what anyone says to me,* she thinks, *I am a child of the King.*

She takes a deep breath and clicks. A few moments later, she exhales in relief. David is baring his heart, relating how he feels about Carrie, telling her he believes the Lord has encouraged him to be open about his desire to pursue a relationship beyond friendship.

That night, Carrie responds with her own e-mail. She has enjoyed getting to know David, looks forward to hearing from him, and loves how he makes her laugh. She says the Lord has assured her that their relationship is a blessing and she also looks forward to a time when they can begin dating.

In April, Carrie and a friend visit David in Amman, Jordan. Carrie and David enjoy an "unofficial first date" that includes a bouquet of flowers from David, an after-hours escape from "tourist police" in an Amman park, and a candlelight dinner. Later during the same visit, Carrie and David drive along a highway near the border to Iraq. They talk about the stories they've heard about what goes on in that secretive nation.

I guess that's one place I'll never know about, Carrie thinks.

Years later Carrie still ponders the irony of her thoughts that evening. Had she known the future, would she have made the same choices? *Unlike God,* she realizes, *we can't see the beginning and the end at the same time. If we could, we might turn back. Since we can't, we trust Him and follow where He leads.*

By fall of 2001, Carrie and David have completed their missionary commitments in the Middle East and live in Fort Worth, Texas, where both are enrolled in seminary. They are free at last to pursue their relationship.

It is an odd time for romance. On September 10, they learn that a good friend and fellow missionary has been killed in a traffic accident in Egypt. The next day brings more shocking and devastating news: Arab terrorists have hijacked airplanes and crashed them into New York City's World Trade Center and the Pentagon. A fourth plane has gone down in Pennsylvania.

September 11 only serves to stir the hearts of Carrie and David even more for the needs in the Middle East. They pray daily for ministries working with Arab Muslims. At the invitation of an area church, David speaks about presenting the gospel to Muslims. He tells the audience that while politics and war are a necessary evil in the fight against insurgency, only Jesus can be the final answer. While their country prepares for battle, so do Carrie and David—but in their own way.

As they pray for Arab Muslims, Carrie and David also pray about each other. David knows he wants to be with Carrie, but he also wants to make sure he acts within God's will. Scripture gives him the confirmation he seeks: "Dear friends, if our hearts do not condemn us, we have confidence before God and receive from him anything we ask, because we obey his commands and do what pleases him" (1 John 3:21–22).

Soon, after many attempts, the words finally tumble out of David's mouth: "Carrie, I feel like we should get married."

Carrie thinks, *What took you so long?* But her answer is more diplomatic: "I came to that same conclusion a week ago." They are married at Lake Highlands Baptist Church in Dallas on June 8, 2002.

Their first year together in Fort Worth is a blur of activity. They love being in America and near family but are homesick for the Arab world. Then, after the U.S. invasion of Iraq in spring 2003, comes an opportunity to return—an invitation to participate in a short-term mission trip that summer.

Carrie and David celebrate their first anniversary by baptizing themselves in a picturesque stream in Iraq. Then David begins to serenade her with old Garth Brooks songs. He sings loud, if not well, and Carrie and their Iraqi hosts erupt in laughter. Carrie cherishes the moment, deeply satisfied that they are finishing a humanitarian project in a country she thought she'd never see, listening to country music sung badly by the man she loves.

Even before the trip is over, David and Carrie are invited to stay on full time in Iraq. The need is great, and the number of volunteers few. At home in Texas, they pray separately for guidance. Both receive the same answer from the Lord: "Go!" Two months later, they are back among the people they so wish to serve.

Both know that Iraq isn't safe. Two aid workers they'd ministered with were recently gunned down in the streets of a northern town. Then the day before their arrival, rocket-propelled grenades slammed into the oil-ministry building and two Baghdad hotels. Carrie and David both harbor apprehensions. But David can't stand sitting on the sidelines, and after tasting life in the mission field, Carrie feels the same way. Besides, as one of their missionary friends put it, they could stay home and "die in traffic in [America]. It's safer to be in the center of God's will." The McDonnalls haven't said yes to an organization. They've said yes to God, knowing He is in control.

Their new home is in a town more than four hours north of Baghdad. Carrie and David quickly go to work, hosting volunteer teams and helping distribute food and nine thousand blankets. They are charged with addressing the needs of the Arab-Muslim population in Mosul, Iraq's second-largest metropolis, as well as an area outside the city.

At first, because of the dangers there, Carrie and David are prohibited from residing in Mosul itself. They quickly become frustrated with trying to serve from so far away. It's difficult to build meaningful relationships among the people of Mosul without immersing themselves in the life and culture there. But the McDonnalls also understand the reasoning behind their superiors' caution. The "Muslim Brotherhood" known as Hamas and the even more deadly Wahhabis are active in the city, frequently carrying out attacks against anyone believed to be linked with the coalition that has taken over Iraq.

Eventually, however, the missions leadership changes its stance. David and Carrie are given permission to begin looking for a home in Mosul. Both are thrilled and sobered by the prospect. The needs are many, but the city's neighborhoods are also home to a number of terrorist organizations. The decision is a matter for much prayer.

David's journal entries from the time are prophetic: "Yes, it's dangerous. Yes, we could die, but Paul faced the exact same dangers, and he faced them boldly, keeping his eyes on finishing his race with joy and being obedient to his call to share the gospel. This kind of boldness is exactly what I need. Lord, give me the boldness to carry Your name to those who may wish to do me harm. Give me wisdom, but more than that, give me courage, strength, and boldness to simply be obedient to hear Your call."

It's March 15, 2004. David and Carrie are still considering the permanent move to Mosul even as they make daytime trips into the area to assess the needs of the people. On this day, they travel in a white pickup truck to check out a camp of displaced people outside the city. They are accompanied by missionaries Larry and Jean Elliott and Karen Watson. It's the last day the Elliotts and Karen will work with David and Carrie before returning to Baghdad.

Using GPS coordinates provided by the U.S. Army, the five-member team locates a paved road that leads to a pair of drab, concrete buildings. Chickens and sheep scurry about in front of the structures. Plain white robes dry on a rope in the afternoon sun.

When they see women peering out from behind curtains, Carrie, Jean, and Karen exit the truck. Following Arab custom, David and Larry remain in the vehicle. Only when some of the Arab men appear do they show themselves.

For more than an hour, the women and men visit in separate groups. "We need water," one woman tells Carrie plainly in Arabic. The people here also appear to be lacking fruit.

The visit takes longer than anticipated. As the missionaries leave, an Iraqi man climbs into the truck with them. Five minutes down the road, the men exit the pickup for another brief assessment at the camp of the Iraqi man's extended family. Finally, the work is completed, and the five missionaries begin their journey toward the relative safety of Kurdish territory south of Mosul.

Carrie is nervous. It's now late afternoon, and they will have to hurry to return before the cover of darkness. Though they could turn off and take a back road to reach their destination, they choose the faster, direct route through Mosul.

As the pickup makes a turn into downtown, all three haphazard "lanes" of traffic suddenly halt. The team is locked between cars. For anyone with the inclination, the five Americans now provide a tempting target, and each of them knows it.

Please, Lord, Carrie prays, *please clear out this traffic so we can keep moving.*

To Carrie, sitting with Karen on her left and Jean on her right in the backseat of the truck's extended cab, everything appears normal. Boxy buildings on either side of the street are covered in a layer of brown dust from the unpaved roads. Businesses are open; people walk along the sidewalks and enter shops. Curtains blow out of second-story windows over the storefronts. There is movement all around the missionary team, but their vehicle is going nowhere.

Carrie fights off the fear. She doesn't want to let her nerves show.

Suddenly, something stings Carrie's right ear.

"Ow!" she cries out.

She raises her hand to her ear. Then, for a moment, the world goes dark.

Carrie revives, still dizzy, and hears David shout from the driver's seat, "Get down! Everybody get down!"

Carrie's heart races. There is nowhere to go.

The deafening roar of automatic rifles fills her ears.

As if in slow motion, Carrie sees it all: six men with AK-47s and at least one Uzi submachine gun surround the truck, guns raised, firing at will into the vehicle. The throbbing, pounding explosive noises go on and on; the scents of metallic gunpowder and blood mix in an awful combination.

Carrie feels bites of pain everywhere. Bullets and shrapnel ricochet off the walls and floor of the truck. She squeezes her eyes shut. She doesn't want to remember the eyes of these men, the hatred behind them.

Jesus, make the bullets stop! she prays. Then she blanks out.

A short time later—she doesn't know how long—Carrie opens her eyes. She's still in the truck. There is an eerie, hollow silence. Outside, what was once a bustling city street is now devoid of life. There is no traffic. The shops appear closed.

The truck is slowly moving forward. With a thud, it strikes a curb and stops.

Carrie looks at her teammates. Jean Elliott, slumped against Carrie, isn't breathing. She's gone. On Carrie's left, Karen is also slumped over, but she's breathing faintly.

In the front seat, David and Larry Elliott are both motionless. *Is David pretending to be asleep?*

Carrie catches sight of her left hand. It's drenched in blood. Fingers are missing. Bones are visible. *Can this be happening?* Remembering her basic first-aid training, she tries to prop her hand up over her heart.

You're going to be fine, a voice whispers.

It can only be God.

"Is my husband alive?" Carrie asks the voice. There is no answer. Carrie doesn't ask again. She's not sure she wants to know.

Everything is hazy to Carrie. She can't breathe through her nose. She knows something inside her isn't right. She feels an object in her mouth, spits it out, and hears a "clink" when it hits the floor of the truck cab.

"Help me," she says in Arabic. It is only a whisper. She tries again, louder. "Help me. Help me!"

Suddenly, David sits up straight behind the steering wheel. "Are you hit?" he asks Carrie.

"Yes. I'm hit bad, David. I have to get to the hospital." She cries out through jagged breaths, "Are you hit?"

"No," he says.

Next to David, Larry Elliott still isn't moving. Carrie thinks he must be dead. *How can David not be hit?*

David steps out of the truck. Carrie watches his eyes take in the horror of a bullet-riddled vehicle full of bodies, blood, and shattered glass. Then he stops and looks her straight in the eye. His intense expression is one Carrie will never forget. It's full of compassion. It's as if he doesn't see her bloodied hand or face. Without his uttering a word, Carrie feels David say, "I'm going to take care of you, just like I swore I would on our wedding day."

David turns to the street. The same loud voice that produced a bad Garth Brooks imitation will now save Carrie's life. "Help us!" he bellows in Arabic. Immediately, men step forward. Carrie hears David rounding them up, explaining that his wife needs to get to the hospital. She closes her eyes in relief. David will handle the situation.

Carrie hears Karen's breathing beside her grow slower and more labored.

Then it stops altogether. Carrie is surrounded by death—drowning in it. Her heart aches at the loss of these good people, at this violent end.

A group of Iraqi men gathers just outside the truck, looking at Carrie. They are here to help, but it is a violation of Arab mores to touch another man's wife. They hesitate.

Carrie looks at David. He's lost color in his face. Suddenly he starts to wobble. "Catch my husband!" she screams. Just in time, two of the men break David's fall.

"My arms and legs don't work," Carrie says to the men in Arabic. "You have to get me out."

The men pick Carrie up and lay her on the sidewalk. The movement triggers an explosion of pain; Carrie screams.

Carrie is wearing a long, loose skirt, per Iraqi custom. Although the skirt is only up to her calf when the men set her down, one of them pulls the hem down to cover Carrie's ankles. It takes only a moment, but in the Arab culture, a man's preserving another woman's modesty is a gesture normally reserved for wives, sisters, or mothers. Grateful for this loving act in the midst of horror, Carrie begins to cry.

Soon Carrie and David are in a beat-up taxi. Carrie is flanked in the backseat by two of her Iraqi helpers. In the front seat, David slips in and out of consciousness, but he's able to place a call to their boss on their satellite phone. "Carrie and I have been hit," he says.

Now Carrie worries about David.

To Carrie's dismay, though the hospital is only a short distance away, the taxi driver stops for gas. *It isn't that far!* she thinks. David and the Iraqi driver open the hood. There's a clog in the gas line; David and the driver jimmy it with a coat hanger to get gas to the engine.

While the tank is filling, Carrie watches another car approach the taxi and slow down. She sees recognition in the taxi driver's eyes. Her heart pounds. *Have the gunmen come back to finish the job?*

At that moment, a truck filled with Iraqi policemen pulls up behind the car. The car speeds away. The taxi, now with a police escort, inches forward again.

Carrie can't think to form a prayer. She just repeats a single name: "Jesus. Jesus. Jesus." David hears and prays for both of them. His voice soothes Carrie.

Several minutes later, they arrive at the hospital. David is rushed in. Carrie's helpers place her on a makeshift gurney outside the taxi as a mob begins to form. After a frighteningly long wait, two hospital employees emerge and bring Carrie inside.

A female doctor assesses Carrie and wraps her hands in bandages. Carrie doesn't relax. She knows they must get to the U.S. Combat Support Hospital unit. In Mosul, one is never completely sure of loyalties—the doctors may fight for your survival or help speed your demise.

Several minutes later, to Carrie's relief, U.S. soldiers appear. "We're not medics," one says. "We're here to protect you until the medics arrive."

Carrie asks a tall soldier named Tim if he believes in Jesus. He answers yes. "Pray for me?" she asks.

Tim calls another soldier over. The soldier drops to his knees at the head of the bed and prays thoroughly for Carrie and David. To Carrie, having a soldier, gun at the ready, pray for her in the heart of this Iraqi hospital means everything. A wave of comfort washes over her.

Nearby, David describes the shooting in detail to the Iraqi police and American soldiers. The doctors, however, are concerned about their patient. They ask for Carrie's permission to insert a tube. U.S. helicopters are on the way; the decision is made to wait.

Five minutes pass, then ten. Carrie learns later that ground fire prevented the helicopters from landing quickly. Iraqi doctors are wheeling David into a room for surgery when the news comes that the choppers are on the ground.

First Carrie, then David are loaded into separate helicopters and transported to the U.S. hospital unit. Carrie can't see her husband when he's wheeled in, but she hears him holler across the hospital, "I love you!" She smiles, tears in her eyes, at the sound of his familiar shout.

"I love you too!" she yells back.

"We're gonna make it through this, baby!" David calls.

"Okay," Carrie shouts back weakly. She sees the questioning faces over her. "That's my husband. He's a good man. You take care of him." She keeps repeating the words. "He's a good man. You take care of him."

As the hospital staff prepares Carrie for surgery, she hears David speaking to the doctors. His voice is getting weaker.

"How's my husband?" she asks a doctor. Seeing Carrie's agitation, the doctor leaves to check.

The doctor returns. "He'll survive."

"Is it okay for me to sleep now?" Carrie asks a nurse. The nurse says yes.

Carrie closes her eyes. Her last memory is of a camouflage-draped ceiling.

Eight days will pass before Carrie is alert enough to keep her eyes open again. She'll be home in America, in a Dallas hospital, surrounded by family. But one of the two great loves of her life will be missing.

Each of the surgeons at the army hospital unit near Mosul believed David McDonnall would survive his wounds. These surgeons were among the best in the business, men who had experience with the worst possible wounds. After they operated on David, they declared him stable and ready for transport, and he was loaded onto a helicopter for a flight to Baghdad. During the short flight, however, David suddenly went into cardiac arrest. He died in the air at 3 a.m. on March 16, 2004. He was twenty-nine years old.

The best explanation Carrie knows for David's death is that it was his time. God had decided to take him home.

Carrie, meanwhile, is trying to make the most of her time. After losing three fingers and on her left hand and enduring ten surgeries, she is able physically to do nearly everything she could before. She has written a book about her life with David and launched a ministry that allows her to speak to groups across the country.

In her appearances, Carrie talks about God's faithfulness. She knows He is a redeemer who can bring good out of any situation, including hers. She sees the evidence firsthand. There was the time, for instance, when she addressed a group of survivors of violence at a breakfast in San Antonio. Carrie connected with her audience as few people could. Afterward, a long line formed; so many wanted to meet Carrie. Often, they had no words, yet the tears in their eyes and their heartfelt hugs spoke volumes.

The dark days don't overwhelm Carrie as often as they used to, but she still desperately misses her husband and mourns the loss of three dear friends.

"I won't sugarcoat the fact that it's been excruciating," she says. "I'm constantly aware of David's absence. I miss our life together. I miss the possibilities of what I thought our future together might hold. I'll mourn for the rest of my life, but I am thankful for the time I spent as David McDonnall's best friend and wife."

Carrie doesn't live with regret. She would never have asked her husband to change who he was.

"David's utmost desire was to be obedient," Carrie says. "He didn't want to be complacent. He knew that sacrifice is sometimes asked of us as believers, but he wasn't looking for ways to give up his life. He never felt called to die.

"David was called to live—and so are we."

NO LIMITS

> For God so loved the world that he gave his
> one and only Son, that whoever believes in
> him shall not perish but have eternal life.
>
> JOHN 3:16

David McDonnall got it. This man was a warrior for God, a guy who knew exactly whom he served and what he needed to accomplish his mission. Look again at his prayer as he considers a move into the terrorist-infested territory of Mosul:

"Yes, it's dangerous. Yes, we could die, but Paul faced the exact same dangers, and he faced them boldly, keeping his eyes on finishing his race with joy and being obedient to his call to share the gospel. This kind of boldness is exactly what I need. Lord, give me the boldness to carry Your name to those who may wish to do me harm. Give me wisdom, but more than that, give me courage, strength, and boldness to simply be obedient to hear Your call."

Is there any doubt that David McDonnall was courageous, strong, bold, and obedient? This is the kind of person our Father wants on His team. David was 100 percent sold out to his Lord. His commitment had no limits.

To me, the Christian life is an adventure—an experience—an experience with God.

David McDonnall

And David wasn't alone. How many newlywed wives would embrace a move into a war-torn nation where going to sleep to the sound of gunfire was routine? Carrie McDonnall is the picture of a woman who stands by her God and her man no matter what. And she wasn't just part of the background. She fully shared David's passion and mission for reaching the lost people around them, despite the risks. In the midst of a dangerous environment, the deep love she felt for God and for her husband flourished, like a candle flame that burns intensely when the wind is just right.

In fact, I can't help wondering if Mosul wasn't the "wind" that fanned the flame of the intense love between God, David, and Carrie. Seeing their obedience despite the frightening obstacles, how could our Father not respond with love? And in the midst of very real danger, how could David and Carrie not draw closer to their God and each other?

Love is often like that. A crisis strips away the protective layers we wear until all we have left is our love for and faith in each other and our Lord.

Stepping obediently into the fire may lead to sacrifice, of course. David and Carrie both understood. David lived out the words of Jesus: "Greater love has no one than this, that he lay down his life for his friends" (John 15:13). The cost of their obedience was terrible—but also temporary. Carrie and David are planning on a joyous reunion in eternity. In the meantime, through David, Carrie now has a greater understanding of the depth of the loving sacrifice Jesus made for her—for each of us—on that cross two thousand years ago.

To live without risk is to risk not living.
Brennan Manning

"My hope still rests in Jesus," Carrie says. "God has been very near, and in His presence I have found the strength to rejoice in His love and faithfulness."

Part of Carrie's rejoicing is watching the Lord touch lives through her ministry. She knows the effect her obedience has had. Her ongoing hope is to one day visit her friends in Israel—and perhaps even Iraq again. But in everything, she is waiting on God and trusting Him to lead, one step at a time. If and when the day comes for her to return, she'll be ready.

David and Carrie McDonnall risked everything to bring the love of Christ to a needy people. They lost so much. Yet they gained even more—a love that outshines it all, on both sides of heaven.

—JL

A Good Day to Die

BY JAMES LUND

Matt Moseley is sitting at a kitchen table, watching CNN news inside Station Four, when the alarm goes off. With each tone, his attention increases. This is a big one.

A radio voice is calling out units: "Engine Ten. Engine Thirteen. Engine Six. Engine One. Truck Twelve. Truck One. Squad Four. Battalion Five. Air Seven. Respond to 170 Boulevard Southeast, cross street Decatur. Reported structure fire."

Moseley and the rest of his squad members jump up and begin gathering their gear. "Sounds like they're sending the whole world out," he says.

Matt Moseley is five foot eleven and 190 pounds, with blue eyes and a blond crew cut. At age thirty, he's the science officer for Squad Four, part of the Third Battalion stationed on Ellis Street in downtown Atlanta. He grew up just a few miles from here, in the small town of College Park, watching the daring rescue efforts of paramedics John Gage and Roy DeSoto on his favorite TV show, *Emergency!*

As a college student, Moseley considered becoming a doctor and enrolled in an emergency medical technician course as a first step. One of the class requirements included a trip to a fire station. That day, when he put on fireman's gear and an air pack for the first time, he forgot all about medical school. He was hooked.

After a few years with the Fayette County Fire and Emergency Services Department, Moseley developed an interest in special operations, situations that demand extra training and skill. Moseley wanted to work with and become one of the best, and he knew that "heavy rescue"—whether it was retrieving someone from a burning vehicle, a river, or a collapsing building—was where he'd be challenged most. After taking courses and completing training, he transferred to the Atlanta Fire Department and its heavier call volume. He was assigned to Squad Four as a specialist in hazardous materials.

Moseley loves and takes pride in his work. He still remembers the admonition of a speaker at a firefighters' conference: "If you go to a grocery store and want a bag of potato chips, you've got myriad choices. If you don't like the bag you've got, you can put it back and pick another one. People who call 911 don't have that choice. You're all they get. How dare you give them anything but your best."

Today, April 12, 1999, Moseley mentally prepares to give his best. The squad is headed for the Cabbagetown neighborhood in southeast Atlanta. Moseley can already see, past the skyscrapers, white smoke billowing across I-75. *It's probably nothing,* he thinks. *Just leaves or trash. It'll burn itself out.*

When the truck arrives, however, Moseley quickly realizes this fire involves more than just leaves. The Fulton Bag and Cotton Mill, a six-story, century-old structure made mostly of wood, is in the midst of a renovation that will eventually turn it into loft apartments. Now, however, it's burning. As Moseley and a group of firefighters from other units run inside, a handful of construction workers make their way out. One warns Moseley about the stairs. "They're rotten," he says. "Watch out for the holes."

Moseley and the rest climb the stairwell. On the huge, open fourth floor, they discover the source of the smoke—a thirty-by-forty-foot area of burning construction scraps and trash. Soon, ladders armed with water pipes reach the fourth floor windows. Several firefighters begin attaching their own lines to the ladder pipes. At the same time, Moseley and Lieutenant Todd Edwards walk around the fire for a closer inspection.

"Look up there!" Moseley shouts, pointing at the ceiling. "It's breaking through the floor!" Flames from the fifth floor are clearly visible through the slats.

"Get up there and check it out," Edwards says.

Moseley drops his ax and hook and runs for the stairwell, where he's joined by Lieutenant Mark Green of Engine Six. Together, they race to the next floor. Three steps into the room, they stop; the heat is too much. From the center of the room, a black fog surges forward, nearly obliterating their view. Still visible behind the smoke cloud, however, is an unmistakable bright orange glow.

Moseley and Green back up. Suddenly, the fire on the fifth floor explodes into an inferno. The voice of the battalion chief, mixed with shouts from the floor below, reaches them from outside the building: "Get out of there! Everybody out!"

When Moseley began his career, he was filled with what he calls "young man bravado, that sense of invincibility." But as the years passed and his tally of close calls rose, he became more aware of the danger, of his vulnerability. He began praying nightly for protection. His faith, Moseley realized, was what allowed him to do what he did. "Guys who have been around—there's a lot of faith there," he says. "God's got a plan for you. If it's your day, it's your day. You just have to go in and do your job. You can't be worried about what I call 'the particulars.' "

Inside the burning Fulton mill, Moseley has no time to consider particulars. He hears the battalion chief's shout, and the next several seconds pass in a blur. He and Green catch up to more firefighters on the fourth floor stairwell. They are the last group in the building, and they're running for their lives.

On the third floor, Moseley hears loud pops and cracks, followed by a deafening rumble. The giant beams directly above him are snapping and collapsing. The heat is intense. *Okay*, Moseley thinks. *There's no way we're staying ahead of this. We're gone.* Almost instantly, and with a surprising calmness, he accepts the inevitability of his death.

But he keeps running.

Second floor. More popping and cracking. The noise is tremendous.

First floor. Like the mill, Moseley's lungs are burning.

Suddenly, a bright light makes Moseley blink. He's outside. He's made it! They've all made it.

Breathing hard, Moseley looks up. The mill's six stories have collapsed into three. Smoke is pouring out of every window. Within fifteen minutes, the entire structure will be gone.

Moseley isn't given much time to rest. Embers from the mill have already reached homes downwind and sparked into flames. The firefighters must evacuate the neighborhood, and quickly.

After a few minutes of going door to door, Moseley and the rest of his squad kneel in the street to regroup. The heat from the mill fire is intensifying; steam rises from water on the pavement. A radio crackles: "We have a rope rescue. Get back to the truck."

On the way, Moseley spots a crowd of firefighters, construction workers, and reporters looking up. His eyes follow their gaze.

Rising above the burning mill is a 220-foot-high steel tower crane. A steel boom crosses the tower near the top; a control cab is attached where the horizontal boom dissects the tower. Moseley can just make out a man's head peering over the edge of the control cab thirteen stories above him. Flames surround the base of the crane and the ladder that leads to the cab.

You've got to be kidding, Moseley thinks.

Monday morning began like any other week for Ivers Sims, a forty-nine-year-old operating engineer for Jasper Construction Company. He got up at 4 a.m. in his home in the small Alabama town of Woodland. Just before leaving for work, he whispered to his sleeping wife, "I'm gone. See ya' later." By 6:30, he was on site at the Fulton Bag and Cotton Mill, where he'd been directing a high-rise crane for the past six months.

About sunrise, Sims began the long climb up the ladder to the control cab. At the top, he stopped a moment to admire the view; it was a beautiful day. He was glad he'd worn an extra shirt, though, as it was a bit chilly. The wind indicator in the cab showed gusts of up to forty miles per hour.

That morning, co-workers shoveled gravel from the mill roof into skids and attached the skids to the crane. Sims's task was to guide the skids to a trash bin. By early afternoon he'd dumped five loads and nearly finished the job. Then he noticed white smoke rising from a three-foot-square hole in the mill's tarpaper roof. Workmen on the roof found hoses and began squirting water into the hole.

The smoke only increased. Sims watched the workers haul the hose down the stairwell and disappear from sight. An instant later, he heard a "whoosh" and saw flames erupt through the roof. Sims picked up his radio: "Y'all got a fire on top of the building."

It was time to leave. But when Sims looked down at the ladder, he saw that the tower was engulfed in flames.

He was trapped.

Moseley and his colleagues discuss the grim situation. They consider shooting a rope to Sims from another building, then realize they don't have a line gun. A firefighter suggests a helicopter rescue. No one can think of another option. Soon Captain Tom Doyle is on the radio with the battalion chief, urging clearance to bring in a helicopter.

"No," the chief responds. "It's too dangerous."

Moseley can see flames turning the base of the crane black. It's an indication the temperature has reached a steel-softening 1,100 degrees Fahrenheit. It is only a matter of time before the crane topples.

Moseley is just behind Captain Doyle when he hears the chief, over the radio, reverse his decision. Later, Moseley says he was "standing in the wrong place at the right time." When Doyle spins around, he nearly bumps into Moseley's chest. Their eyes lock.

"You're going," Doyle says.

Moseley swallows. For the second time this day, he's facing his mortality, and the feeling is distinctly uncomfortable.

I've never done anything like this before, he thinks. *This would be suicide. Should I back out? Should I say, "No way"?*

Moseley shakes his head. *If I'm gonna say that, I better get into another business, because my business is being a firefighter.*

Moseley recalls a line he heard once: a firefighter has only one brave moment in his life, and that's when he takes his oath of office. Everything he does after that is in the line of duty. Moseley realizes he committed himself to what he's about to do a long time ago. He's a firefighter, and his duty is to rescue others.

Moseley begins pulling out gear. It's time to get ready for the helicopter.

Like Ivers Sims, Boyd Clines figured he was in for another routine week. He'd been on vacation, returning Friday to his home in Douglasville. His wife,

Deidre, woke him on Monday at 8 a.m. before leaving for her job at the local high school. Soon after, he drove himself to work at Fulton County Airport.

Clines, fifty-two years old and a slender six foot one, is a pilot for the Georgia Department of Natural Resources. He's been flying helicopters since the army taught him how at age nineteen. He's rescued soldiers from jungles and swamps in Vietnam and Cambodia. He's survived two crashes and a "hot" landing in Laos that nearly destroyed his instruments and got him a bullet through his leg.

More recently, he's pulled people out of floodwaters and canyons in Georgia. He's a man who's learned how to keep cool under pressure.

On April 12, at 3:25 p.m., Clines has just completed a visual inspection of the department helicopters when the distress call comes in: someone needs a chopper to pull a man off a crane.

Clines and Larry Rogers, his mechanic and crew chief, shift into emergency mode. They pop the back doors off N35NR, a Bell Long Ranger L-4, and load coiled nylon ropes and a Billy Pugh rescue basket into the cabin. They also strap a green "belly band" made of nylon webbing around the floor and underside of the Long Ranger. Then they throw on their flight suits.

Less than ten minutes after the distress call, Clines and Rogers are airborne.

Ivers Sims is getting hot. He's already climbed out of the cab and onto the steel counterdeck above it. He's also said a prayer. Electricity to the crane is out, and the wind has whipped it around so it's pointing south.

Now Sims is feeling intense heat through his boots. He keys his handheld radio. "Hey, Keith," he says to his superintendent, "when's that helicopter coming?"

"They're gonna get it here quick as they can," the superintendent replies.

The heat keeps rising; Sims needs to move. Quickly, but carefully as possible, he makes his way away from the tower along the catwalk to the short end of the boom, where eight concrete slabs serve as counterweights to the boom's long end. The concrete is cooler than the steel. Sims lies on his stomach. His world has shrunk to a few feet of concrete in the middle of the sky.

It's time, he decides, for another prayer.

Three helicopters appear. Two move in his direction but back away before they get anywhere near him. The third, a news chopper, inches closer than the others, apparently hoping Sims can climb aboard. But the heat is so great Sims can't even stretch his arm past the edge of the concrete. The news helicopter pulls back.

Sims considers the very real possibility that this is his last day as an engineer for Jasper Construction Company.

On the ground, Matt Moseley is wearing a harness under his turnout coat. A traffic copter on loan from a news agency lands in a nearby grassy area next to a cemetery. *That's fitting,* Moseley thinks. *A graveyard.*

Moseley and his team discuss how the rescue should play out. They decide that one firefighter will be lashed into a seat in the chopper and will prop his feet against a bulkhead. A second firefighter will also be tied in and will use a rescue rack to control tension on the rope as he lowers Moseley down.

When he looks in the eyes of his fellow squad members, Moseley sees doubt. But what else can they do? They can't just watch a man die.

The firefighters are boarding the traffic helicopter when another chopper lands. Moseley sees the belly band and realizes this aircraft is already rigged for rescue.

"That's what we need!" he shouts. He jumps out of the first helicopter and runs to the new one. Quick introductions follow. The rotors of N35NR are still whirling overhead, so everyone has to shout to be heard.

Pilot Clines and crew chief Rogers had intended to lower a basket to Sims, but Moseley is concerned that Sims won't be in any condition to climb in. "If he grabs at the basket and misses, the whole thing'll be over," he says.

Clines raises an eyebrow. "Okay, if you wanna take the ride," he says. "Let's go. Time's wasting."

Take the ride? Moseley doesn't understand. His plan is to rappel out of the chopper and down a rope to reach Sims. Moseley climbs into the helicopter, but Rogers, standing outside, shakes his head and waves him out.

"Come with me!" he yells.

His brow furrowed, Moseley follows Rogers to a point several yards in front of the chopper. Rogers is carrying fifty feet of nylon rope connected to another thirty-foot length with steel carabiners. One end of the rope is attached to the belly band. Rogers points to Moseley's harness. "Hook the rope right here," he says, "and we'll take care of the rest."

Now Moseley gets it. They expect him to dangle from the rope for the entire rescue! Suddenly, his mouth is dry. He can feel his tongue swelling.

He takes a deep breath. *Okay,* he thinks. *Let's get this done.*

From the cockpit, Boyd Clines sees Moseley give a thumbs-up. Their radios are incompatible, so hand signals are the only way to communicate. "All right, Larry," Clines says. "Help me get Moseley off the ground—gently but surely."

Rogers leans out of the Long Ranger and plants a foot on a skid step. Clines slowly lifts off. He's been on the ground for just seven minutes.

Clines can't see Moseley as the chopper moves upward, so he listens carefully to Rogers. They rise twenty feet, then thirty, then fifty. Soon Clines feels a tug from below. Moseley is in the air. He keeps guiding the helicopter higher. "He's cleared the light poles," Rogers says. Then, "He's cleared the wires. Ease forward now."

As a pilot, Clines has participated in plenty of rescues, but never downtown in a major metropolis, and certainly never with a human being swinging under him over a fully involved blaze. He knows this mission will take precision and every ounce of his concentration.

Clines guides the chopper in a sweep around the crane. Sims is still on his stomach on the concrete. Clines can't tell what shape he's in. Sims's former location, the cab, is in flames. The crane itself seems to be moving with the wind.

They don't have much time.

―――――

As the helicopter rose above him, Moseley walked slowly forward until he was directly beneath the chopper. Seconds later, the harness tightened around his body and lifted him into the air.

Now, more than two hundred feet above the ground, Moseley feels an unexpected peace. The only sound is the whirring of the helicopter rotors and pops and cracks from the flames below. *What a beautiful day it is,* he thinks. *What a fire. For a fireman, this is some sight.* He's distinctly aware of how easily this mission could take a bad turn, but he's accepted it. *If you're a fireman, this is a good way to go. This is a good day to die.*

When the Long Ranger moves over the burning mill, hot air rises to greet Moseley. The sense of peace fades. He peers into the blazing black shell of the mill. *This,* he thinks, *is like looking into hell.*

The helicopter and Moseley move down, closer to the crane and the fire. Moseley feels a series of small stings all over his body; his skin is beginning to burn. He hides his face in the collar of his turnout coat.

We need to speed this up.

―――――

In the cockpit of the Long Ranger, Clines is also dimly aware that the heat is building, but he can't think about that now. His eyes are fixed on his instruments. With Rogers as a guide, Clines inches the aircraft closer to the crane and Sims.

"Down to the left," Rogers says. "A little down and back. Now a bit to the right."

Under normal conditions, a helicopter hovers close to the ground, where the pilot can see the horizon and use it to help him maintain a stable position. Now, however, Clines has only smoke and sky as visual aids. He's totally dependent on Rogers.

Another advantage of hovering close to the ground is the added lift from air that's driven down by a chopper's rotors, which then rebounds off the ground. At three hundred feet in the air, however, Clines has no additional cushion. To maintain position, his engine speed is at top capacity. "The engine can't hold this for more than four or five minutes," he tells Rogers.

"We're still a hair away," Rogers says. "Down a little. Left. Left. Left!"

Moseley is dangling within twenty feet of Sims, who's now sitting up, motionless, on the concrete. "Don't panic," Moseley yells. "Don't grab for me. I'll do it all. Just stay put." Sims doesn't reply.

As the Long Ranger guides Moseley closer, the rope turns, rotating Moseley so his back is to Sims. Moseley twists and waves his arms, trying to turn around, with no success.

I gotta turn, he thinks in frustration. *I gotta turn. I'm never going to be able to do this if I can't turn!* Though gusts have been blowing all day, now there is no wind whatsoever to help him.

Suddenly, Moseley experiences a strange sensation, as if someone has put a hand on his leg. The "hand" gently nudges him 180 degrees, until he's facing the concrete slabs and Sims. With his own gloved hand, Moseley grabs a cable on the crane. He hoists himself onto the steel catwalk.

"He's on! He's on!" Rogers yells to Clines in the Long Ranger. "Careful—he's still hooked up."

This isn't what Clines wants to hear. He expected Moseley to unhook from the rope as soon as he reached the crane. Instead, with Moseley still connected, Clines must maintain a near-perfect hover. Too much slack, and the rope will wrap around the crane. Too little and the helicopter will lift Moseley into the air again, potentially throwing him against the crane or bouncing Sims off and into the flames below.

Lord, Clines prays, *we've got to do this right. We can't make any mistakes. You're going to have to help us pull everything together in the next few minutes.*

With waves of heat washing over him, Moseley steps along the catwalk toward Sims. To Moseley, the bespectacled engineer waiting quietly appears calmer than his rescuer.

For the second time that day, Moseley is warned to be careful of his footing. "Watch out," Sims says. "There are holes." Moseley looks down. He notices black footprints—the residue of Sims's melting boots when he walked across.

In a few seconds, Moseley joins Sims on the concrete. As he's been trained, Moseley tries to break the tension with a joke. "Hey, your boss sent me up to tell you that you can knock off early today." Sims just looks at him. *Okay, no more jokes,* Moseley thinks.

"I need to put this harness around you," Moseley says. "Just let me hook it up. You can sit and let me work, and we'll be out of here in just a second." He wraps a webbed harness around Sims and secures it to a carabiner on the rope above his head. With a second carabiner, he attaches Sims to his own harness.

Moseley has been on the crane for two minutes. He raises his head and flashes a thumbs-up.

In the cockpit of the Long Ranger, Boyd Clines is completely focused on the hand controls of the helicopter and the voice of Larry Rogers inside his headset. Clines doesn't notice the heat warping the protective bubble at the front of the chopper.

"They're ready," Rogers says. "Bring 'em now. We got 'em."

As gently as he can, Clines eases his craft higher. Every second feels like a year.

"Slow," Rogers says. "Slow."

Clines is barely breathing. Once again, he feels the tug on the rope as Moseley and Sims are hauled into the sky.

Moseley has his arms around Sims, whose head is about three inches below the firefighter's. After a brief attempt at small talk, Moseley understands that Sims isn't in a chatty mood. Together they admire the amazing view: the buildings that make up downtown Atlanta, the blazing inferno, the crowds of people, the grave sites inside historic Oakland Cemetery. Moseley hears cheers and applause from below. It's an exhilarating feeling.

Two minutes later they gently touch down on grass and are surrounded by a happy mob of firefighters and paramedics. Sims is unhooked and whisked away on a stretcher. He's treated at Atlanta Medical Center for smoke inhalation and heat exposure and released that night. Later, during a television interview, Sims is ready to talk. "Thank you, Matt," he says. "Thank God for your courage and bravery. I'm going to change your name to Moses, not Moseley."

At the landing site, meanwhile, firefighters pound Moseley on the back in celebration. His throat is so dry he can barely speak. One squad member offers him a cup of water, but Moseley's hands are shaking so badly he can't get his gloves off to hold it.

Moseley pushes through the crowd to reach the helicopter, which has landed in the grass next to the cemetery. Clines and Rogers are already surrounded by media. It's an odd scene—print and television reporters jostling for position amidst smiling firefighters, the rotors of the Long Ranger slowing but still spinning, and just beyond the whirlwind of activity, the gray stone wall of the cemetery. It reminds Moseley of the closeness of death. Twice in the past few hours, he nearly experienced it firsthand. But this day, as it turned out, was not a good day to die.

Moseley greets his two new friends, the pilot and the crew chief, with a simple phrase: "The first round is on me." With the rescue complete, he feels obligated to buy his partners a drink. It's a ritual, another part of his duty. But then his professional veneer is replaced by a wide, relieved grin. Duty is important, no doubt about it, but the satisfaction he'll take home from this day will mean much, much more.

MEETING GOD

> Come near to God and he will come near
> to you.
>
> JAMES 4:8

It hit Boyd Clines the night of the rescue of Ivers Sims. The more Clines watched TV news footage of the dramatic events over the Fulton Bag and Cotton Mill, the less he observed his own actions and the more he saw God's invisible hand steadying his own. As on so many of his most dangerous flights, there was a brief time when a power greater than his own intervened. Once again, Clines couldn't see any other explanation for it. God was on the scene.

For Moseley, the realization took longer, but it struck him with just as much force. He thought about his precarious position below the helicopter when he'd been twisted the wrong way. There were updrafts from below, but no side wind whatsoever. His own efforts were futile; he couldn't turn around. Then he'd felt as if something physically touched him and gently pushed him into just the right position.

"I didn't think there was any way," Moseley says now. "That had to be God turning me around. Only He could have done that, and only He could have brought all the right people together— Boyd being an expert pilot, me knowing just enough to be dangerous, Larry Rogers doing his part, and Ivers being so calm—to pull off that rescue."

Neither Moseley nor Clines describes himself as someone who often experiences spiritual encounters. Both are practical, logical, industrious men who take pride in their work and their steady reliability. And both are convinced they met God in the air over a burning mill that spring day in downtown Atlanta.

Could it be that when we are bold enough to step away from our safety nets and into the "fire" of God's call, this is when we're most likely to encounter Him? Is living in the hard places the quickest path to meeting and growing a relationship with the Almighty?

In fact, the Bible says as much. Noah endured scorn and ridicule to build an ark. David went to war with a slingshot because of his faith. Paul risked his reputation and his life, turned away from a career of tormenting the followers of Christ, and emerged as one of the leading apostles. In each case, and in examples throughout Scripture, these

> *From one man [God] made every nation of men, that they should inhabit the whole earth; and he determined the times set for them and the exact places where they should live. God did this so that men would seek him and perhaps reach out for him and find him.*
> Acts 17:26–27

men found themselves in the Lord's presence. They gained a new nearness to God and a deeper understanding of His power and love.

I have at least a small idea of what they experienced. Four years ago, I rejected the advice of a few trusted mentors, walked away from a position with a publishing company, and started a freelance career. To some, it wasn't a smart move and certainly not the safe thing to do, yet I sensed it was the direction God wanted me to go. Since then, my business has grown steadily. What's more important, though, is that it has changed my relationship with the Lord. I've found myself depending on and

> *The place that God calls you is the place where your deep gladness and the world's deep hunger meet.*
> Frederick Buechner

growing closer to Him. I'm reminded daily of His nearness. My new career has turned out to be one of the scariest—and best—choices I've ever made.

Matt Moseley says that since choosing to take his "ride" in downtown Atlanta, he's discovered a new sense of humility and is less likely to take God for granted. He's also gained faith in his ability to respond in a crisis. Next time, he says, he'll be even more prepared—and more ready to meet God when he's at the end of his rope.

—JL

I Want to Live

BY JAMES LUND

Sunshine glints on Brian Shul's helmet visor as he emerges from a nondescript van and steps onto a gray tarmac. It's a bright morning at Kadena Air Base in Okinawa, Japan, even brighter than the gold spacesuit the U.S. Air Force major wears. Shul climbs thirteen feet up a metal stairway, shakes hands with his "backseater," Major Walt Watson, and slides into the sleek metal beast before him. He's in the cockpit of "The Lady in Black," otherwise known as the top secret SR-71 Blackbird spy plane, one of America's premier intelligence-gathering resources and the world's fastest and highest-flying piloted jet.

Shul and Watson's mission on this spring day in 1985 is an orientation flight. They're to become familiar with the local flying area, emergency landing sites, and restricted areas. The majors are expected, of course, to follow their flight plan to the letter. No one ever alters the mission. Too many dollars and too many lives are invested in the Blackbird program for pilots to "John Wayne" it.

Except this time, Brian thinks. Today, he has a personal matter to address.

Brian sits in front of an array of consoles and switches more complex than any he's seen in nearly twenty years as a pilot. Technicians have already provided water bottles and maps and clicked every switch in the cockpit into proper position, but Brian and three members of the ground crew go through the checklist again to make sure. Soon, powerful Buick V-8 engines in an external "start cart" are firing, followed by what to Brian, wearing a nearly soundproof helmet and cocooned inside the cockpit, is a resounding thump. To everyone outside the jet, the moment when the jet fuel in the powerful twin J-58 engines ignites is a deafening explosion.

With the jet now pulsing around him, Brian feels a familiar rush of excitement. The Blackbird is alive again.

Minutes later, maintenance personnel pound chocks out of the way with sledgehammers, and the crew chief flashes a thumbs-up. Brian taxis the SR-71 onto the runway. When the Blackbird appears, everyone around and beyond the borders of the base stops what he's doing to watch: Marines servicing a P-3 submarine tracker scramble onto its wing for a better view; taxi drivers momentarily ignore prospective customers; golfers hold off on lining up putts. Brian radios his status to a controller in the Kadena tower. Then he gives Watson a warning.

"Uh, Walt," he says, "we're going to have a slight deviation in our takeoff today."

Watson appears unruffled by this unprecedented announcement. His response is a single word: "Okay." Brian suspects Walt knows what he's up to. He mutters a prayer of thanks for his understanding partner.

Watson counts down the seconds to takeoff. At zero, Brian releases the brakes and presses the throttle forward. Like a racehorse being released from its chute at the start gates, the Blackbird surges ahead. Five thousand feet later, traveling at over 240 miles per hour, it begins rising into the air.

In seconds, Brian sees it—before the ocean and the beach, about a mile past the runway, is a five-story white building surrounded by athletic fields. Instead of moving higher and making the subtle left turn indicated by his flight plan, Brian stays low, about three stories above the ground, and banks left. The Blackbird roars past the building and fields. Grade-school kids stop their soccer games to view the thunderous creature above them. Brian moves the jet into a hard right and pushes on the throttles, sending it into a steep climb for the sky. It will be an impressive show for the kids in the fields and anyone who happens to be watching from the windows of the white building.

Brian knows the view from those windows well. It was on the other side of those windows that he confronted the greatest fear of his life. Now, soaring high above them, he is overwhelmed by a feeling of intense satisfaction. *Eleven years,* he thinks, feeling the tightness of the scars on his right hand as he moves the throttle. *Seems more like a lifetime.*

9:30 a.m.
April 11, 1974

Brian Shul is a twenty-five-year-old air force lieutenant helping train South Vietnamese, Thai, Laotian, and Cambodian pilots in advanced combat techniques near the close of the Vietnam War. He also, as a member of a special-ops wing, flies covert missions that will never be officially recognized by the U.S. government.

Brian has already completed one sortie, a routine patrol near the borders of Laos and Cambodia. He figures he's done for the day. But as Brian walks out the door of the squadron building on the large base in northern Thailand, the scheduler calls out, "Hey Shul, we need a quick flight down near the Cambodian border. The Special Forces guys want some cadmium batteries."

Brian groans. "I'm tired," he says. "I'm ready to go home."

The scheduler persists. "We'll give you the fastest plane on the ramp. Just there and back. You can be done by one o'clock."

Brian hesitates. He doesn't want to go. But the guys in this particular Special Forces unit are his new buddies. A few weeks before, Brian and eleven other pilots accepted their challenge to join them in a three-week fitness course. It meant waking up at four in the morning to run five miles, lift weights, perform endless pull-ups, and endure a creative variety of insults, all before beginning the day's regular duties. Of the pilots, only Brian and one other lieutenant finished the course.

It had been a grind, yet Brian felt it was worth it. He loved meeting a challenge. Now he was in the best shape of his life, and he'd earned new friendships and respect from both the Special Forces team and members of his own squadron.

With the scheduler waiting for an answer, Brian gives in. *It'll be easy,* he thinks. *Just get down there, land, dump the batteries in the baggage pod. It's a milk run.*

The Vietcong have recently stepped up their presence near the Cambodian border, but Brian doesn't give that a second thought. He knows that risk is just part of the job of being a fighter pilot. As an instructor, he tells his fellow pilots, "Don't climb into that cockpit unless you're right with your family and God, or whatever you believe in, because every time you fly, you risk everything you ever were or will be." Brian isn't married, but since childhood he's put his trust in Jesus Christ. Climbing into the cockpit, he's never felt alone.

Soon Brian is preparing for another cockpit visit; he begins a flight check on a stripped-down AT-28D. This trainer-turned-fighter is only thirty-three feet long, straight winged, driven by a single propeller, and rarely flies faster than 250 miles per hour. But it's proven its worth as a close-air support aircraft in Vietnam and has been good to Brian during several months of missions.

Brian inspects the hydraulic ports, flaps, and weapon stations. He checks the engine, smearing oil on his black gloves. Satisfied, he climbs onto the wing and into the cockpit. Just fifteen minutes after starting his flight check, Brian signals the crew chief that he's ready. There are no gold astronaut suits in Thailand; Brian still wears the olive green flight jumper, now stained with sweat, which he put on earlier that morning. The suit has no identifying name, rank, or other insignia. It allows U.S. authorities the option of "deniability" if Brian goes down in the wrong territory.

Just after 10:00, Brian hurtles down the concrete runway in the AT-28D, pulls on the throttle, and glides over a thick, green jungle canopy. It's a beautiful day in Southeast Asia; not a single cloud is visible. Despite his fatigue and the fact that he's in the middle of a war, he can't hold back a grin. There's nothing quite like the view of a jungle from a fighter plane at five thousand feet.

A half hour later, Brian begins to lower his altitude for the approach to the remote base. Everything is going smoothly. But it takes only an instant for a routine flight to transform into a matter of life and death.

When Brian presses on the throttle, the plane suddenly fails to respond. Brian presses harder; no change. The throttle no longer affects the engine.

Brian's heart rate jumps. *Well, this isn't good.*

He doesn't panic. He's been in critical situations before and always found a way out of them.

For the next thirty seconds, Brian runs through every trick he knows to restore the connection: shifting the throttle position, remixing fuel flows, restarting power sources. This time nothing works. The engine is still running, but Brian has no control over it. What he doesn't know is that a minute earlier, Vietcong hidden in the jungle shot several rounds of small-arms fire into the belly of his AT-28D, severing the link between the throttle and engine.

Brian rapidly weighs his options. *Eject? No, they took the seat out of this one. Should I just bail out? No—I'm too low. I'll get impaled on a tree.*

The AT-28D keeps descending. It's flying at two hundred miles per hour. The top of the jungle canopy quickly grows more visible.

I'm going to hit the trees. At least the propeller's still turning. Got to keep it level so I don't cartwheel.

He picks up his radio. "Tiger 18 declaring an emergency," he says. "I'm not going to make the runway."

Brian concentrates on balancing his wings. The jungle is close now, maybe a hundred feet below. He flies over rolling hills and ravines. He can distinguish individual trees as they whiz by. The plane's speed is down to 150 miles per hour.

Brian looks down and grimaces. He's always been a confident pilot. The fear that attacks him now is strange and unwelcome. His guts feel like hamburger in a meat grinder.

This is going to be really bad.

He radios a final, terse message: "Tiger 18 is in the trees."

A few seconds left—not even time to pray. Suddenly, certain that he's going to die but just as sure that God is with him, an amazing sense of calm washes over Brian. The plane seems to move in slow motion as it falls the final few feet.

It hits.

Brian's calm is shattered by an unearthly, earsplitting shriek as the jungle tears at the AT-28D's fuselage and wings. The single propeller churns through the thick foliage, trying in futility to forge a path through the greenery. Dark, twisted shapes, like tentacles from the deep, slash at Brian's body. He feels as if he's being torn apart.

The shrieking and slashing seem to go on forever.

Abruptly, all is silent.

I'm dead.

In that instant, time seems suspended. Images flash before Brian: people at his grave site shaking their heads; newspaper headlines announcing his death. For a moment, Brian is somehow above the plane, observing his lifeless body in the cockpit. He is calm about his death, yet terribly sad.

All of a sudden he's back in the plane. He feels his soul trying to rise out of his body, but another, more powerful force pushes it back down. Though it's not audible, Brian hears what feels like a voice: *No. You're not dead. You need to deal with this.*

The images and voices end. Brian is alive and inside the cockpit. It's unbelievably hot; he feels pain all over.

I'm on fire, he thinks. *I've got to get out!*

The cockpit of the AT-28D sits directly over the fuel pumps, which ignited the moment the plane crashed. Brian is being roasted alive. He can't see because the fire has melted the exterior visor on his helmet, and now the interior visor is beading up. Instinctively, he holds his breath. From memory, he unhooks the belts and harnesses that hold him. He punches the canopy release button, which to his surprise still works.

Brian stands, but something tugs him back toward his seat. He realizes the quick-release microphone cord has melted to his helmet. With adrenaline pumping at maximum, he grabs the cord with both hands and rips it in half.

Still nearly blind, Brian leaps onto the left wing and scurries to the tip. It's close to a ten-foot drop to the jungle floor, but there's no hesitation. He jumps, rolls on the ground, scrambles to his feet, and runs.

About a hundred yards away, reeling from burns and shock, Brian collapses. He throws his helmet off, lies on his back, and puts his feet on top of the helmet.

He's numb; the pain isn't intense yet. But he can see he's badly burned. Nearly everything is black and charred on his torso and from his fingers to his shoulders. He thinks he's still wearing his flight suit. He doesn't realize he's looking at what's left of his skin.

Our Father who art in heaven, hallowed be thy name...

Brian silently utters the Lord's Prayer.

His face feels stiff. He realizes he has no control over his hands.

I'm gonna die right here.

Brian lies still. The only sound is mournful pops and crackles from the burning AT-28D.

Through gaps in the trees, he can make out patches of blue. *Good. If I'm going to die here, Lord, at least I'll be able to see the sky one more time.*

Brian prays and waits. An agonizing hour passes. Finally, another sound reaches his ears—distant voices speaking in English.

"Lieutenant Shul! Can you hear me? Lieutenant Shul!"

It's his Special Forces buddies. They've found the wreckage of the plane, but they're looking for him on the wrong side.

Brian tries to cry out, but no sound comes from his mouth. He can barely move his jaw.

My God, he thinks. *If they miss me, I'm not going to last out here.*

He takes a deep breath and tries again. The best he can manage is a whisper.

He prays for strength. He's almost in tears from the frustration and effort. Finally, after several long breaths, he croaks out a shout: "Over here!"

Someone says, "This way!" A minute later, a soldier appears. It's John, one of the guys from the fitness course, wearing a helmet and green fatigues and carrying a rifle. John is as big and tough as they come, six feet four inches of hard muscle, trained for battle in the harshest of conditions.

When John sees Brian, his face contorts. He turns away and pukes.

More soldiers surround Brian. One cries. Working quickly and quietly, they rig a stretcher and move Brian to a clearing.

"Water," Brian whispers.

One of the men pushes a piece of wet gauze into Brian's mouth. It provides little relief.

Finally, a few minutes later, a helicopter lands to take Brian to a hospital in Thailand. There, doctors with somber faces cut off the remains of his gloves and flight suit, apply disinfectant, and bandage him.

A few minutes after they finish, a chaplain enters the room and begins to administer last rites.

Brian feels the fury rise inside him.

"What are you doing here?" he shouts, his voice still a raspy whisper. "I'm not ready to die yet. I'm not even Catholic. Get out of here!"

That night, paramedics prepare Brian for another flight, this one to the hospital at Kadena Air Base. It's where the military sends soldiers injured in Vietnam who aren't expected to make it.

Brian spots some of his friends from the Special Forces unit peering through the doorway. In their eyes, he can see sadness and pain.

A few minutes later, at the airfield, Brian's squadron lines up on the tarmac to send him off. As the paramedics wheel Brian to a C-9 transport, some recoil and turn away.

What's the matter with these guys? he thinks.

A light drizzle begins falling as Brian reaches the ramp to the plane. The moisture in the air is barely more than mist, yet each drop on Brian's face feels like a steel spike being hammered into his skull. It's the first time Brian begins to understand the extent of the burns all over his body.

His ordeal has only just begun.

"Aaaaaaaaahhhh!"

The shout comes from another burn patient in the next room. Brian, however, doesn't have the strength to scream. The only sound he makes comes from grinding his teeth, followed by breathing so fast the nurses wonder if he'll pass out.

If only he could.

Brian lies naked in a whirlpool filled with a saline solution. He's surrounded by five hospital technicians, one at each arm, each leg, and his head, all armed with scalpels. They are performing a procedure known as debridement—the surgical removal of dead and contaminated tissue from the body. It is marked by scrubbing, ripping, cutting, and pain.

In previous treatments, hospital staff administered the highest possible safe dosage of morphine to Brian, but it did nothing to ease his agony, so they gave it up. Brian endures the treatments without painkillers of any kind. The staff must end each treatment after twenty minutes; otherwise, their patients run the risk of dying from shock.

Every morning, starting at 6:00, Brian endures another round of torture. The doctors at the naval hospital in Okinawa tell him he's lucky to be alive, that only a young man in peak physical condition could have survived. The inside of his body is in surprisingly good shape; by holding his breath in the cockpit, Brian protected his internal organs.

The outside, however, is another matter. Third-degree burns cover his face, neck, arms, hands, thighs, and part of his torso. His body, unbandaged, looks like a slab of red meat at a butcher shop. Doctors drive long steel pins into each finger to keep his hands from curling into useless appendages.

Brian has no appetite. He was once a taut 175 pounds. Now he's 119 pounds of water, blood, and gauze.

Every day Brian wakes up and, through the window beside his bed, views a glorious red fireball rising out of the Pacific Ocean over an Okinawa beach. To anyone else, the sight would be breathtaking, but to Brian, the light signals death. When the sun rises, it means they'll soon be coming for him again.

You may have a plan here, God, Brian thinks, *but You've got the wrong person. I can't do this. There's no sense going through all this. It's going to kill me. I thought I was tough. I thought I was strong. I admit it—I'm not. Please just let me die.*

Day after day, the sun keeps rising and the treatments keep coming. Finally, Brian has had enough.

It's 3 a.m. Brian lies alone on his back in the dark, bandaged and unable to move, inhaling a foul combination of disinfectant, blood, and pus. To his left is the closed window. To his right is an IV machine on a pole. A thin tube snakes from the IV into his arm.

I'll never fly jets again, Brian thinks. *No woman will want to date me. I'll never be able to enjoy eating again. I'll never go hiking because I can't be in the sun. I'll never be strong enough to do sports again. Everything that was fun in my life is gone. I'll just be a freak.*

Brian is in despair. He believes he no longer has anything to live for or anything to offer. He's looking at his future and can't bear what he sees. This is far worse than the fear he experienced in the cockpit before his crash.

He's terrified.

God, I don't want anyone to see me like this. I don't want to live like this. Please let me die.

He rolls his eyes to the right and takes in the IV machine just a couple of feet away. He focuses on the gray lever that regulates the flow of nutrients keeping him alive.

If I could turn that switch, he thinks, *I could sleep forever.*

Brian closes his eyes to concentrate. His bandaged right arm, unsteady, rises an inch, then another. Putting all his energy into lifting his arm, Brian manages to raise it six inches into the air.

The effort is too much. The arm falls back down. Brian blinks back tears. He doesn't even have the physical strength to kill himself.

Three hours later, the first hints of orange appear in the window.

The sun is rising.

A few days later, Brian is still in his room, distinctly uncomfortable. Every breath hurts. To distract himself from the pain, he asks a nurse to turn on the small black-and-white television on the shelf across from his bed. There's only one channel, with broadcasts by the Armed Forces Radio and Television Service.

Today's choice, a week before Easter, is a French production of the Easter story and the crucifixion of Christ. There are no flashy special effects, but the simple presentation of the familiar tale draws Brian in. It's as if he's experiencing it for the first time.

When Jesus is nailed to the cross, the intensity of the moment overwhelms Brian. He watches and listens to a Roman soldier pound nails into Jesus's hands. Brian shudders at the sound of each hammer blow. He looks down at his own bandaged hands, which still contain steel pins.

For the first time, he understands.

Jesus may have been supernatural, but He did feel it, Brian thinks. *Up on that cross, He was just a man, feeling pain like I'm feeling pain. He willingly did that for us.*

A couple of days later, Brian is listening to Armed Forces radio. It's a beautiful day outside, sunlight glimmering on the ocean. The windows in Brian's room are usually closed to prevent infection, but he talks a nurse into opening one a crack. He feels like a caged tiger.

On the radio, Judy Garland begins singing her classic rendition of "Over the Rainbow" from *The Wizard of Oz.* Brian has heard it a hundred times, but never paid much attention to the words. This time, trapped in his hospital bed, he listens closely:

Somewhere, over the rainbow…dreams that you dare to dream really
do come true.

The lyrics penetrate Brian's mind in the same way the nails pierced the hands of Christ. *That song is about believing, about following your dreams,* Brian thinks. *That used to be me! I used to be a motivated, positive person. What's happened to me?*

From the barely ajar window, Brian hears birds chirping and the shouts of kids playing soccer in the fields below—a place far removed from his own world of heaviness, pain, and death.

I'm still that positive person inside, he thinks. *I've just had my external shell rearranged a little bit. Even if I can't fly again, I can still be productive. I don't want to just give up.*

In that moment, Brian lets go of his fear of the future. He doesn't know what's ahead. He doesn't know if he'll be able to regain even a fraction of his former life. But he's determined to find out.

He has a new challenge to meet.

Brian still dreads the rising sun. He still grits his teeth and suffers during his burn treatments. Yet somehow they seem a little more bearable.

Two months after entering the Okinawa hospital and having endured thirty-two burn treatments, Brian gets good news: he's being transferred to the burn center at Fort Sam Houston in San Antonio, Texas. The doctors foresee a long road ahead—two years of surgeries followed by three years of physical rehabilitation—but Brian doesn't care. He's going home.

While recovering at Fort Sam Houston, the air force sends Brian paperwork for a medical discharge. Brian returns it unsigned. It happens a second time, then a third time. Finally, a colonel from air force headquarters in San Antonio makes a personal visit to Brian and his surgeon. The colonel then sends over the air force's chief of flight surgeons, a tall, white-haired colonel in a blue uniform.

Brian explains why he won't sign the documents.

"I'm not ready for a medical discharge," he says. "I want to find out if I can fly again. I'd like to at least try. No one's even giving me a chance to try."

The chief studies Brian's face. Finally, he speaks.

"I like your attitude," he says. "You tell me when you're ready for that physical. I will not be easy on you. I won't give you any breaks. But if you pass and I sign off on it, there's not a doctor in the air force that will dare question it."

Both the doctors at Okinawa and the air force personnel staff have underestimated Brian. He endures fifteen difficult surgeries and an intense regimen of physical therapy. But nine months after he arrives at the Texas burn center, Brian takes the air force pilot physical and passes. Three hundred fifty-two days after his arrival at Sam Houston, he walks out under his own power. Two days after that, he climbs into the cockpit of a T-38 for a training flight, part of his new assignment at Holloman Air Force Base in Alamogordo, New Mexico.

Brian is back in the saddle. Physically, the accident has left him with occasional sharp pains in his hands, back trouble, and severe scarring on his face, neck, arms, and thighs. But internally he's as strong as ever. And his attitude toward life has changed dramatically.

Brian's brush with death and the long journey back to a productive life have removed his fear of failure. He no longer worries about what people think about him. He isn't concerned about going broke or looking foolish. *What could be worse than what I've already been through?* he thinks. *People who give up on their dreams or don't even try are dying a slow death. I want to live.*

Over the next few years, Brian pilots A-7 fighters, flies in the first operational A-10 squadron, and teaches at the Air Force's Fighter Lead-In School as the chief of air-to-ground academics. Though he's never been a public speaker, he also begins accepting invitations from veterans groups, businesses, churches, and medical groups to talk about his life. The response is encouraging.

One day at the Cleveland National Air Show, Brian hears over the public-address system that an SR-71 will soon be making a low pass over the field. Brian has never seen the Blackbird in person, so he scrambles up into the cockpit of his jet for a better view.

The SR-71, 107 feet long and capable of flying at three times the speed of sound, arrives exactly on time. Even without weapons, its elegant form and sleek profile command respect. When the pilot raises its wheels and pushes both throttles to full afterburn, its power and speed are quickly revealed. From half a mile away, the sound of the Blackbird's engines vibrate the canopy on Brian's jet.

Brian is impressed.

In 1983, Brian informs his superiors in Tactical Air Command that he wants to volunteer for the SR-71 program. They discourage him. They don't want to lose their investment in a talented pilot.

But Brian persists. He takes his case to a general, a former racquetball partner. The general agrees to give Brian a chance.

Because the Blackbird routinely cruises at altitudes above eighty thousand feet, pilots are required to pass an astronaut physical. Brian's medical history and scarred exterior may give the test administrators reason to doubt his chances. But on the inside—physically, emotionally, and spiritually—Brian is stronger than ever. He takes the physical and scores the highest mark of any applicant in the previous four years.

Over the following four years, Brian serves as a pilot in the SR-71 program, gathering intelligence for the United States in flights over sensitive areas around the globe. Three of the most important of those missions occur during a time of escalating tensions between the United States and Libya, which includes accusations of Libyan support of terrorists.

On April 15, 1986, Air Force F-111s and other U.S. aircraft strike targets in Libya. Brian and Walt Watson are in the air in an SR-71 when they encounter the F-111s on their return flight. Watson counts the jets as the formation passes below. They're one short. One crew won't be coming home.

Brian and Walt pass into Libyan air space, the supersensitive cameras on the bottom of the SR-71 recording every inch of territory beneath them. Brian knows that on this day, the Libyans will be especially unhappy about their presence. Sure enough, Brian soon hears Walt's calm voice in his headset: "They've launched a missile at us."

Brian pushes the twin throttles forward. Speed is their only weapon against the attack from below.

Moments later, Watson speaks again: "More launches. Push it up." This time Brian hears tension in his partner's voice. The threat is real.

Brian presses the throttles full forward. The Blackbird, as if relieved to finally be let loose, smoothly accelerates past mach 3.32, then 3.35, then higher. The jet's speed is approaching 2,500 miles per hour. It's the fastest Brian has ever flown.

The seconds tick off. Brian and Walt need to hit the scheduled turn in their flight plan before the missiles hit them.

Brian sneaks a glance out the window. It's highly unlikely he would see the missiles before they strike, but the view of clear sky still makes him feel better.

Finally, the Blackbird roars into its turn and begins its departure from Libyan air space. Brian lets out a long breath. Mission accomplished. He's done his part this day for the cause of freedom.

Brian feels intensely satisfied, a sensation he once thought he'd never experience again. He thinks back to his first assignment as a fully certified SR-71 pilot—two years earlier at Kadena Air Force Base in Okinawa.

On his first off day at Kadena, Brian returned to the site of the white navy hospital building he remembered so well. He walked to the soccer field below what was once his third-floor window and sat on a bench. He bent over and pressed his hands into the grass. A breeze touched his scarred face. He watched the children play. They weren't the kids he saw and heard eleven years earlier, but they made the same happy sounds, innocent and unafraid.

On the bench that day, Brian held his head in his hands and wept.

That very first flight—the one with the course deviation that took him and Walt past that same white building—was the most satisfying flight of all. That's when Brian realized he'd come full circle. It was his love of flying and meeting challenges, along with the bullets of Vietcong snipers, that led him to Okinawa eleven years earlier. And it was that same love of flying and meeting challenges, this time in the fastest and most elegant jet of them all, that brought him back.

In between, he'd lost something—his body wasn't what it used to be.

But I've gained so much more, Brian thinks, his mind back on the flight home from Libya. *I'm choosing to live my life. I wouldn't trade that for anything.*

Brian nudges the throttles, keeping the SR-71 on course. It races on through the cobalt blue sky, into the great beyond and a future waiting to be discovered.

THE GREAT AFFECTION

I trust in God's unfailing love for ever and ever.
PSALM 52:8

As a U.S. Air Force fighter pilot in Vietnam, Lieutenant Brian Shul
was a man who faced death on a daily basis. No one would have
even thought to question his courage. He believed in his training
and abilities and in his God. Confident and committed to the
cause, this was one guy who had his act together.

Yet the Lord knew this military man's weak point. Through
a fiery crash in the jungle and the terrible fire that baked the flesh
off his body, God allowed Brian to lose everything. His career. His
confidence. His looks. His ability even to care for himself.

Brian was scared—terrified, really. All he had left was his faith
and a choice. He was at the turning point of his life. Would he give
in to the fear that swirled around him like a Kansas tornado? Or
would he give himself completely to the Lord and discover a deeper
courage than he'd ever known before?

Brennan Manning has written, "When we are seized by the
power of a great affection, we are empowered with the courage to
risk." The "great affection" seized Brian as he lay helpless in a hospital bed, watching the story of Jesus on the cross, hearing—and
feeling—each strike of the hammer that drove in the nails. Brian
already knew that his Lord cared for him. But this time he understood that he was profoundly *loved.* More intense than the worst of
the burns that covered his body, that discovery seared Brian's soul.

Scripture tells us that "Perfect love drives out fear" (1 John
4:18). It is the kind of love that enabled Peter and John to risk con-
fronting the religious leaders of their day (see Acts 4:18–20), that
allowed Stephen to ask for mercy for his tormentors even as he was

being stoned (see Acts 7:60). It is the same love that encouraged Brian to risk climbing back into the cockpit, to seek missions flying the world's fastest jet, to take on a new career as a public speaker, photographer, and author.

"God had a plan for my life," Brian says. "I can't take the credit. It's Him, and I'm along for the ride. I'm thankful every day. So often, I think, we miss life. I've found that most people don't do half of the things they want to do. They're afraid of failure, of how they'll look, of what people will say, of not being accepted. But what's the worst that can happen? You fail. You fall down. You go broke.

"Some people are intimidated when I say that. They'll say, 'I don't know. That's kind of scary.' But it's scarier doing nothing."

Doing nothing means sitting in the boat when Jesus calls us to Him. I wonder if our entire lives are encapsulated by the account of Jesus and the disciples on the Sea of Galilee (see Matthew 14:25–33). Jesus walks on the water, moving toward us. We shrink back in fear. He calls out, "Take courage! It is I. Don't be afraid."

Most of us, at that point, choose to stay in the boat. A few of us, like Peter, step onto the water and begin to walk. Then, so often, we again give in to fear and begin to sink. Yet Jesus, demonstrating His perfect love, pulls us out and gently asks, "You of little faith, why did you doubt?"

> *Courage is not the absence of fear, but rather the judgment that something else is more important than fear.*
> Ambrose Redmoon

We doubt, of course, because we know He's not safe. Because sometimes He takes our eyes, our skin, our loved ones, our freedom, and even our lives. Yet when we risk in order to grow personally and spiritually, when we step out of the boat to meet our Creator, we choose *life*—a life that can never be lost. When we stay in the boat, on the other hand, we lose something. Sitting there, we're already on the path to death.

The mountaineer understands the choice. Sooner or later, every climber confronts a decision point like Peter's, a move that's uncertain. You're not sure how deep the crack is above you. You wonder if that next foothold can hold you. You're so scared your knees are knocking. But to get to the top, you've got to act on faith and make a "commitment move."

That's what Peter did—he made a commitment move. He wasn't sure about this walking on water business. But with the encouragement of Christ, he conquered his fear and stepped out of the boat. Yes, for a moment he lost his nerve. But he ultimately found a new confidence, a greater courage, one that would eventually lead him to the life he was intended for, including unimaginable deeds of glory for the kingdom.

God never promises to fully erase our fears. His promise to us is that He'll walk beside us, encouraging us to make that next move—and if we sink or fall, the Great Affection is there to offer His hand.

—PJ

Deeper into Mystery

BY BRUCE HENDRICKS

Our life is a faint tracing on the surface of mystery.
ANNIE DILLARD

Distant and indistinct, I hear the guttural rumblings of another avalanche pulling loose somewhere in the valley. Four of us are approaching the base of Slipstream, a three-thousand-foot ice climb on the north face of Mount Snowdome in the Canadian Rockies. After a brief pause, I continue kicking steps in the snow up and across the forty-degree slope toward the base of the ice.

I stop suddenly as I hear an echoing from walls across the valley. As the rumblings grow ominously louder, I am sick with awareness of what's approaching.

Oh no. Run! MOVE!

Struggling, knee-deep in snow, I look up, certain of what I will see. The black rock band above me rears upward to meet a stark blue sky, hiding the huge alpine face; but I know there is more. With frightening speed, a white wave of snow explodes into view. In surreal slow motion, airborne chunks of angular ice rush toward me, beautifully highlighted in the rich morning sunlight. Understanding now that I cannot reach shelter, I hurl myself facedown onto the slope, desperately sinking the shafts of both ice tools and furiously kicking my boots into the soft snow.

The wait is agonizing. I can feel the sparkling chill of snow beneath my face slowly melt as it contacts my warm skin. *Why is this taking so long?* I am grimly certain about the brutality to come. Barreling down a prehistoric limestone reef, a tidal wave of snow is about to wash my existence away. It will bury me alive, or it will effortlessly sweep me from the face and hurl me into the nether world below, a world of icefalls, crevasses, and dark mystery.

In less than two seconds, I have prepared to die. *Let's get on with it.*

When the debris finally hits, the violent impact crushes the wind out of me, twisting and distorting my body. Shrieking ice meteors smash into my pack, then into my fragile limbs. I experience a surge of adrenaline—one last, sweet rush before death. Unexpectedly, a sudden resolve to live floods through me—muscles clench, my inner being intends to fight.

Resonating through my stomach and chest, the slope vibrates with shock waves, shuddering under the impact of debris falling from three thousand feet above. The force wrenches me downward, but strangely, I feel it through my harness. Suddenly, I think of Sheila, my wife, on the other end of the rope; we were moving *together* across this snow slope! Panic engulfs me.

I can visualize the debris slamming into her, catapulting her down the slope until the fifty-five feet of rope between us is exhausted. I imagine her dangling like a rag doll on the end of a string, taking hit after hit.

My own panic evaporates as I come alive with new motivation to save my wife. Yet I can't break free from the gruesome tether attached to my harness. The rope yanks at my waist with incredible force, pulling me downward toward the confusion. My feet plow furrows through the snow. Blinded, face-down in whiteness, I come to a surprising stop. The rope is still taut. Somehow, I have held Sheila.

If only it were over.

Caught in the impact zone, I feel the white waves continue to pound on me. Finally, the random collisions begin to recede, their sound and fury muffled by the growing load of snow under which I lie trapped. Now, squeezed and submerged in suffocating darkness, I wonder how long I can hold my breath. All my strength and will cannot cause my chest to expand. This is it.

Then, like Moses' parting of the Red Sea, the burden of snow that pins me in place slides off, allowing air—and hope—to rush in. Exposed and confused, I struggle to understand what has happened. I should be dead by now.

Before my thoughts can be completed, I am hammered by another onslaught of debris. Again, the violent beating is followed by pressure, suffocation, and darkness. This second surge completely buries me before I realize the tugging at my harness has disappeared. Somewhere, somehow, in the maelstrom below, Sheila has found shelter. Perhaps one of us will survive after all.

That or the rope has broken.

This can't last, I think. *I can't last.*

But it does—and I do. More impact, more violence, more suffocation. And then…grace. A long moment of emptiness with no sound, no impact. The contrast is overwhelming. Cautious, suspicious, I nudge my head and shoulders up through the surprisingly shallow layer of snow; nothing but stillness and a gentle dusting of snowfall.

In an adrenaline-induced daze, I stand up and look out into an ocean of white. In front of me, billowing snow crystals cloud the air like steam. Slowly, blue sky bleeds through the fog. Tentatively, the morning sun and its warmth return. With them, life seeps in. Deliberately, but urgently, I begin to walk down the slope, wondering where Sheila is, knowing full well it may not yet be over. I half expect a blast of disaster to hit me from behind: the finishing touch.

Within moments I hear voices, first distant, then closer. Sheila and our climbing partners, Mike and Geoff, come into sight round the corner, ready to dig for my body under tons of debris. While trying to knock out the compressed snow stuck between my head and helmet, I greet their incredulous looks with an anemic smile and a subdued greeting: "I think I'm ready to go home."

Shaky, I prop myself against a sheltering rock wall while all three fill me in on their experience. Geoff's diabetes had necessitated a short respite to shoot up some insulin and down a bit of food to fuel his blood sugar. It was a fortunate stop. While they were packing up, sheltered beneath the rock band, I continued above. When the rope stretched tight, Sheila began moving up the snow slope as well. An instant later the wave launched itself from the top of the face; by the time Sheila saw it, it was too late. As she tried to run for safety, she was caught from behind and hurled down the slope.

During a momentary lull, Mike and Geoff peered out from their sheltered stance to see a battered Sheila dangling from the end of the rope just a few feet away, plastered in white, looking like a wedding cake decoration. Once again, Geoff's timing was impeccable. He reached out, grabbed Sheila, and pulled her to safety beneath the sheltering wall. Immediately, the torrent roared to life again, erasing the impressions left in the snow by Sheila's body.

When the avalanche's roar fell silent, Sheila, unable to see me, shouted up. No answer. The three of them were expecting the worst when they came around the corner to search for me.

Sheila's first thought when Geoff yanked her to safety was, *What a kind thing to do.* She'd had similar feelings toward another friend who'd saved my life when I slipped, unroped, at the top of a crag in California. That day, I slowly slid headfirst over glacier-polished granite toward an overhanging drop, and our friend Paul (Geese) Giesenhagen dove down the slabs to save me from going over the edge.

Here on Snowdome, I have come perilously close to the line a second time. My leg is aching from a hit, so I stop for a moment. From my vantage point, I see chunks of ice and snow littering the slopes below us for eight hundred feet to the moraine. I can't believe *tons* of that stuff actually landed on me. The thought fuels a surge of adrenaline. We agree to take it easy on the descent; we don't want any screw-ups now.

Plunge-stepping down the scoured snow, winding my way through crevasses filled with fresh debris, I'm plagued by questions: *Why did it happen? What set the avalanche off?* We had planned so diligently, monitored the conditions all season, and turned back on several previous attempts. Over the past three years, we had started out no less than five times to do the route. Twice we'd turned around due to warm, unsettled conditions; one of those times the route had avalanched after we safely reached valley bottom. A friend with the warden service who monitored avalanche and ice conditions told us they were the best he'd seen in several years. We certainly hadn't been rash.

I desperately want things to make sense in a way I can understand, analyze, evaluate…justify. But this doesn't make sense. The avalanche is completely unjustified.

As I hobble down the crest of the moraine, my emotions blister into rage. My anger is a reflection of my own powerlessness. Part of me thinks I should have been able to control or at least assess all of the factors involved. Like Adam in the garden, I am engaged in a twisted deception. I think I am the one in control, that God is holding out on me, that I should be sovereign. But I'm not. Despite our best efforts, we almost died. I am furious and frustrated. We should never have come this close. I am utterly amazed we survived. It all seems wrong.

My leg and arm soon throb their way into my awareness. The pain reminds me how fragile the gift of life is and how strangely thankless I am to be alive at the moment. I am overflowing with self-reproach, bitterness, and a sense of being victimized. Things did not go according to plan.

Imagine both of us killed at the same time! Kern and Logan would have been orphans!

I fume all the way to the bottom, and I am still seething when we reach the gravel flats below the moraine. Even my vision is affected. A vague but persistent distraction invades the margins of my awareness. I look away and gaze down the valley. As I do, an arresting image takes form in my peripheral vision; it's one that has visited me before.

Poised on the edge of my perception, an ethereal, arched doorway hangs motionless in the sky. It is no more than a thought, but its purpose is clear. It is an entryway into another place. The door leads to a world both alluring and frightening, a realm few willingly visit but one that all must eventually explore.

The door hangs slightly ajar…and it beckons.

My anger and self-pity fade as I wonder what mysteries lie on the other side. From my side of the doorway, I can just make out voices mingled with laughter. More distant and indistinct is the sound of music. I am suddenly inundated with longing—loss and sadness mixed with a strange tinge of joy. The now-familiar voices bring back powerful memories, visions from the past…

Our footsteps echo off the pastel walls and freshly waxed floors of Banff's Mineral Springs Hospital as we walk toward Matt's room. Turning the corner, I see him sitting on the bed. It serves as a reality check. He is alone. His face is cut and scabby. Dark purple bruises mottle his face and arms.

"Hi, you guys. Come on in." Matt's slight drawl reminds me of his southern roots. He is as cordial as ever.

Our five-year-old son, Kern, is with Sheila and me. He knows Matt's wife,

Julie, has been killed in the fall that injured Matt. They had only been married a few years. I don't want Kern to be insulated from death, but I don't want him to be overly exposed to it either. Kern listens as Matt describes how he and Julie were swept fifteen hundred feet down the Aemmer Couloir on Mount Temple, bulldozed by a collapsing chunk of overhanging snow.

Kern's nervous and silly behavior tells me he doesn't quite know what to make of it all. Neither do I.

"Just before we were hit, Julie looked down at me and said how great it was to be in the mountains doing what we loved and doing it together," Matt says.

He and Julie had climbed numerous alpine routes together in South America, Canada, and Alaska. Having guided with him in Ecuador, Sheila and I both knew Matt was careful and aware. He had been the only one of his party on Dhaulagiri, an 8,000-meter peak in the Himalayas, to turn back when they encountered high avalanche conditions; he was willing to make the hard call. Because of that, his next statement hits me with force.

"It's one of those things that we all know can happen," he says. "It's a roulette game when you venture into the alpine."

I cringe from the arbitrariness of that image. Doing something that is both random and potentially fatal with someone you love doesn't seem reasonable to me. I reassure myself that the risk can be moderated by careful planning, judgment, and skill, that God's sovereignty and purpose are at work whether I recognize it or not—

Matt's voice cuts my thoughts short.

"I don't know if you guys remember," he says, "but you met Julie down at the guides' meeting in Yosemite Valley a few years ago. After we talked with you, she commented on how she admired you two for all the things you were able to do together in the mountains. She set her sights on developing a similar kind of lifestyle."

In hindsight it struck me as a bittersweet success. The goal that Julie strove for and achieved gave her life, but it also took life from her—and from Matt.

Where is God in all this? I wonder. The real and eternal consequences of human choices—Julie's choices, my choices—leave me profoundly unsettled. I sincerely want the eternal to be comfortable, to spare me struggle.

As we leave the hospital, Sheila and I talk with Kern. Sheila asks if he is ever scared when she and I climb together. He says yes, sometimes he is.

"What are you afraid of?" Sheila asks.

"I'm afraid you might die."

Before I can reassure Kern with a touch or a word, the vision begins to fade, lost to its own wispy rhythms. For a fleeting moment, I'm back in the Rockies, back on Slipstream. Then another apparition appears in the doorway…

My friend Bill and I are ambling along the Toby Creek trail, watched over by tall stands of fir and spruce. Here in the clouds, sunshine, and forests of British Columbia, we're working a wilderness-based professional-development course together.

We soon become engrossed in one of the deep, personal conversations that so characterize Bill. Mostly we talk about the importance of relationships and our thoughts about death. Bill is no stranger to the transition beyond this life. In Britain he has been actively involved in mountain rescue, repeatedly observing the outcome of adventure gone wrong. He has also climbed on big peaks in the Himalayas, where the statistical chance of dying is greater than that of a soldier's in war. On one occasion, while traversing a massive snow slope, Bill watched, horrified, as an avalanche swept past him, carrying several teammates to their deaths. They had been no more than ten steps ahead of him.

"I've seen friends and family die lingering deaths, incapacitated and in pain," Bill says as we walk along. "When I die, I just want to up and go."

Bill notices that we've hiked past the location where we had intended to stop. While I stand and listen to the murmurings of the creek, Bill heads back to find the spot where we want to meet the others. It is a beautiful day: breezes through the trees, dancing water, drifting clouds dappled with sunlight.

Suddenly, from behind, I hear a groaning-growling sound. I turn round, half expecting to confront a bear. Instead, I see Bill lying outstretched on the ground, forty feet away.

As I rush over, Bill is shaking with convulsions; his eyes are fixed and stare right through me. Though he has a pulse, he's breathing in fitful gulps. I open his airway and monitor his vitals, all the while talking to him as I normally would. I begin praying too. In a strangely appropriate way, it all seems an extension of our conversation on the trail.

It isn't long before things change. First, Bill's breathing stops. Then I lose his pulse. I perform CPR, compressing, breathing, counting, all the while conversing urgently with Bill and with God. *Lord,* I pray, *I know You are all-powerful and that if You desire Bill to recover, stand up, and start dancing, You can do that; I would like to see You do that.*

I am afraid—afraid that God will not do that, that what God wants and what I want are not the same.

After twenty minutes I am pretty sure of the outcome. On Bill's chest, in the place where I rest my hands for compressions, a depression has developed. His skin has lost its elasticity. He's changed color, from ashen to light blue. It doesn't occur to me to stop.

An hour later I am on the phone with Bill's wife, Karen. Sobbing, she desperately wants to know what happened. Though I can describe the events, I can't explain the reason for them. Bill had been vibrantly alive one minute, then crumpled and dying in the trail the next. I slump against the pay phone, devastated. Bill's son Tony is entering his teen years, and Karen has just beaten cancer. In many ways their lives were just beginning. With a click of finality, I hang up the receiver. This hasn't turned out the way I'd hoped, the way I'd prayed...

Like Karen's voice, the vision of my last hours with Bill grows dim, then ceases altogether. A bit disoriented, I slowly come to my senses beneath the sky and the silent peaks of the Canadian Rockies. The suspended doorway has vanished. Standing on flat, windblown snow, I gaze up at Slipstream's shining form draped down the face of Snowdome. Chunks of debris still lie scattered over the slope reaching to the moraine. Everything around me feels dreamlike. So many things have turned out different from how I think they should have.

I look around. Sheila and the others have continued on and are nowhere to be seen. I feel small and utterly isolated. The memories of people from my past are set like characters upon this landscape—characters that are beyond reach. Unbidden emotions rise from internal burial places—sadness mostly, and feelings of being cheated. Cheated out of time with people I wanted to know better or laugh with more or climb with once again.

But among my ghostly feelings are recollections of joy as well, shared experiences with those once-tangible voices: conversations over coffee, drives up the Icefields Parkway between Banff and Jasper, evening phone calls to lay plans—ordinary moments, memories that elicit pleasure and longing. Which of those voices will I have the opportunity to talk with again on the other side?

Today it could have been Sheila who passed beyond reach, or me—or both of us. Instead, we were left at the doorstep. It is too much for me to fathom. In one sense I can grasp salvation, grace, sovereignty. But when confronted with the reality of God's hand at work, I sometimes think—like Adam, like Job, like countless others—that I could have done a better job.

Do I trust God? Do I believe Him?

For what seems a long time, I sit quietly and try to soak it all in. I find it hard to simply *be,* to *experience,* to *accept.* I try to create some thread of meaning, piece together an understanding, impose my sense of what should be on the reality of what is. I am anxious for those beyond the door. I am clear that the other side includes not only joy but also darkness and alienation. This uneasiness profoundly disturbs me; I wish it would go away, but I know it will not. My thoughts and feelings drift, weaving themselves amongst the voices and the distant music—prayers given voice and blown by the Spirit's wind, each one transformed into an offering.

Finally, my time at the doorstep seems complete. Without knowing exactly how long I've been here, I slowly stand up and renew the descent. My friends' voices have receded beyond hearing, but a new rhythm gradually grows to take their place. It is the music, the singing, I heard faintly spilling from the door.

The melody plays over and over inside my head. I have no desire to drive it away. The music brings a peace that calms my agitation. I am not sure about the situation for those who have stepped, or been pulled, through the doorway, but I know there are consequences and comfort. I know their choices matter.

And mine. And God's.

As I approach the road and the waiting car, I slowly reenter the world of the familiar with its distractions and diversions. It feels as though I have awakened from a dream within a dream. There is much I do not understand, but I walk the path with Him who does.

I do believe! Help me in my unbelief.

There remain callings here on the familiar side of the doorway to which I have not yet responded. The fragile gift of life has been renewed—life together with Sheila, with family and friends, surrounded and indwelt by God's Spirit. It is a precious wakefulness that lies wrapped in folds of the eternal. Still, in its time, there remains one further awakening: the passage through the doorway.

SURFING SLIPSTREAM
by Sheila Hendricks

I float.
The wings of dawn are warm aglow
Crisp air beneath my feet
Each breath is lightly blown aloft
Then grief.

An ocean weight of snow descends,
Black day.
A puppet on a slender thread
I bear the blackness and the dread
Dance limply to the rhythm of my fate.

I'm cleansed.
Death waits in place
A mundane part of consecrated life.
I've borne this weight
Then paused, exposed
To let the darkness offer Light.

ON THE DOORSTEP

> The vision comes and goes, mostly goes, but I
> live for it, for the moment when the mountains
> open and a new light roars in spate through the
> crack, and the mountains slam.
>
> ANNIE DILLARD

The mountains cracked violently, and the roaring light burned, but that day on Slipstream was one of life's rare moments for Bruce Hendricks. An experienced and widely traveled ice climber, Bruce has come to treasure those instances of awareness of and encounter with the Divine. They deliver a clarity of purpose and priorities like nothing else in our existence. They can also be painful in ways that go far beyond the physical.

Bruce said later, "Those moments defy and define me, revealing that I am not God. Perhaps more importantly, they confront me with how absurdly often I allow myself to slip into that delusion, acting as though I have the right and clarity to dictate how things should turn out. Too often I respond with anger instead of appreciation, frustration instead of acceptance, condemnation instead of grace, hubris instead of humility."

I have an idea of what Bruce is talking about. My own adventures—most recently my bout with cancer—have exposed me to those moments as well. I've wrestled with setting my own agenda for the character and quantity of my years before submitting (and resubmitting) it to Him. And as Bruce

> *He who forms the mountains, creates the wind, and reveals his thoughts to man, he who turns dawn to darkness, and treads the high places of the earth—the LORD God Almighty is his name.*
>
> Amos 4:13

describes in his story, I too have sat on the doorstep and found myself peering through, wondering about friends already there and my future on the other side.

Do I fully understand all of this—my place and purpose in the universe, the God who created me and guides me still, what it means that I have chosen to love and belong to Him now and into eternity? I have an inkling of the answers from the wisdom of Scripture, from the love and compassion I've experienced in this life, and from each truth glimpsed during my adventures. But the mystery remains. I suspect that what I actually comprehend of God's wonder and plans for me is like a single grain of sand on a vast beach. There is so much more waiting to be discovered. I won't find the answers until I step through the doorway—and even then, there may be more mysteries to unfold, more dreams to capture, more adventures to live.

I hope so. The thrill of exploring, of seeking and discovering, has brought me the greatest fulfillment and taught me the most lasting lessons on what matters. It is a gift from God that I deeply treasure. It is hard for me to imagine that He will remove this gift when I step through the doorway.

I am beyond content with my earthy existence; I cherish it. Like Bruce, I have more to do in this life, more callings to answer. But I know my time to join those on the other side is coming, and I will be ready when the moment arrives. It is the next great adventure, one that promises new risks, deeper rewards, discoveries I cannot imagine, and an incredible relationship with my Lord.

Am I excited about that? You'd better believe it.

—PJ

WHERE THEY ARE NOW

GIL MCCORMICK recently took a sabbatical from his position as general manager of Wheat Ridge Cyclery in Wheat Ridge, Colorado, to launch a trip around the world with Leona and their three children. In his words, they "departed on a trip out of the matrix of the everyday to explore the American West, chase the sun around the world, and see where the Spirit leads us." STEVE VAN METER is a partner with Clifton Gunderson, a national CPA firm. He and his wife, Donna, live in Centennial, Colorado, and have two children in high school, Eric and Emily. Steve recently climbed Mt. Rainier with Eric and continues winter ascents of 14,000-foot Colorado peaks. JIM NOWAK is cofounder and executive director of the dZi Foundation (www.dzi foundation.org), which provides basic health care and education to people in remote regions of the Himalayas. Jim lives in Ridgway, Colorado.

DAVE AND BARB ANDERSON still live in Arizona and are completing their thirty-third and final year of Christian concert ministry. They are working on a twenty-year vision of establishing a counseling center for hurting and burned-out couples in the clergy. Dave and Barb firmly believe that the Lord is their "God of rescue" from the Bering Sea and from the pressures of ministry.

CHRIS BRAMAN continues to live in Alexandria, Virginia, with his wife, Samaria, and three daughters. He is pursuing medical retirement from the U.S. Army and studying for a bachelor's degree in information security system computer science. Chris speaks frequently around the country about his experiences on 9/11 and his faith in God. (To schedule an appearance, e-mail cbraman@earthlink.net.) SHEILA MOODY is a staff accountant for the Department of Defense at Fort Meade, Maryland. She is the mother of three adult children and lives with her husband, Vincent, in Maryland. Two months after 9/11, Sheila was able to thank her surprised "guardian angel" in front of a national television audience on the *Oprah Winfrey Show.* The Braman and Moody families remain friends to this day.

BRUCE OLSON is the author of *Bruchko* and *Bruchko and the Motilone Miracle*, which relate his experiences as a missionary living among the Motilone Indians for more than forty years (see www.christianlifeministries.org). He continues to spend most of his time with his friends in the jungle on the border of Colombia and Venezuela.

TED ROBERTS is a pastor at East Hill Church in Gresham, Oregon, and the author of several books, most recently *Going Deeper* with coauthor Pam Vredevelt. He is president of Pure Desire Ministries International, a ministry that helps men and women free themselves from sexual bondages. Ted and his wife, Diane, also present Sexy Christian seminars across the nation and recently appeared on television's *Good Morning America* to promote the seminars to unchurched audiences.

CARRIE MCDONNALL is the author of *Facing Terror,* which tells the story of her and her husband's life and ministry together, and is the founder of Carry On Ministries (www.carryonministries.org). She continues to work in missions by challenging God's people with her testimony and by encouraging them to look beyond themselves to see God's true purpose for their lives. She lives in Texas.

MATT MOSELEY received the Medal of Valor, the highest national award for valor by a public safety officer, for his efforts in rescuing Ivers Sims. He continues to serve with the Atlanta Fire Department's special operations unit, Squad Four. He is also co-owner and CEO of GSM Training Associates, which conducts rescue training programs for the fire service and military. Matt is married and is the proud papa of a two-year-old daughter. BOYD CLINES also received a Medal of Valor for his part in the downtown Atlanta rescue, as well as the Georgia Peace Officer of the Year Award for Valor and (with Larry Rogers) the Aircrew of the Year award from the national Airborne Law Enforcement Association. The father of two grown daughters, he recently retired from his job as a pilot for the Georgia Department of National Resources and lives with his wife, Deidre, in Douglasville, Georgia. LARRY ROGERS is still an employee of the Department of National Resources.

BRIAN SHUL is a professional photographer, speaker, and author of five books, including *Sled Driver: Flying the World's Fastest Jet* (see www.sled driver.com). As a keynote speaker, his inspirational talks have motivated audiences nationwide. Brian owns Gallery One in Marysville, California, where the full collection of both his aviation and nature photography is displayed.

THE HENDRICKS FAMILY (Bruce, Sheila, Kern and Logan) recently returned to Canada after five years in Australia, where they helped lead several outdoor programs. They were involved in a small Anglican church in Kangaroo Valley, a rural town south of Sydney. Bruce was part of a small men's group there that proved a powerful means of growth and support. The Hendricks now live south of Calgary in Alberta, where Bruce is director of outdoor education for Strathcona-Tweedsmuir School. Climbing (rock, ice, alpine), mountain biking, and skiing continue to be their outdoor activities of choice.

NOTES

Introduction
John Eldredge, *Wild at Heart* (Nashville: Thomas Nelson, 2001), 5.

Chapter 1: One Good Shot
Photo: Peb Jackson (left), Denver Darling, and the Cape buffalo felled by Peb's .375 H&H Magnum in the Zimbabwe bush.

Robert Ruark, *Horn of the Hunter* (Long Beach, CA: Safari Press, 1987), 22–23, 285.

Chapter 2: Remember Leona!
Photo: Gil McCormick on Pumori about a week before the final summit push. The peak in the background, left, is Ama Dablam.

Robert Sullivan and Robert Andreas, *The Greatest Adventures of All Time* (Des Moines, IA: LIFE Books, 2000).

Jon Krakauer, *Into Thin Air* (New York: Villard, 1997).

Everest and K2 summit and death statistics from Ed Douglas, "Over the Top," *Outside,* September 2006 and "Everest vs. Big Mac—killer statistics," www.mounteverest.net/story/stories/EvrstvsBigMa-killrstatistis Mar22004.shtml.

Gil McCormick, Steve Van Meter, and Jim Nowak, interviews with the authors.

Gil McCormick's private journal of the climb on Pumori.

Henri Charrière, *Papillon* (New York: Harper Perennial, 2006).

Chapter 3: Bering Sea Rescue
Photo: Cary Dietsche (center) is transported to Norton Sound Regional Medical Center with the help of Kevin Ahl (left) and Randy Oles.

Story adapted from Dave Anderson with Norm Rohrer, *The Rescue* (Tempe, AZ: Fellowship Publishing, 1995). Used with permission.

The Rescue Story, video (Tempe, AZ: Fellowship Publishing).

David Anderson and Barbara Anderson, *Rescued by the Hand of God,* CD (Colorado Springs: Focus on the Family, 1996, 2004).

Dave Anderson, interviews with the authors.

C. S. Lewis, *The Lion, the Witch and the Wardrobe* (1950; repr., New York: HarperCollins, 2005), 80–81.

Chapter 4: Guardian Angel

Photo: U.S. Army Ranger Sgt. Chris Braman with daughters Lauren (left) and Courtney at Fort Myer, Virginia, on the day he is awarded the Purple Heart and Soldier's Medal for his actions on 9/11.

The 9/11 Commission Report (New York: Norton, 2004).

Gail Stewart, *America Under Attack: September 11, 2001* (San Diego: Lucent, 2002).

Joseph A. Gregor, "Air Traffic Control Report," *National Transportation Safety Board,* December 21, 2001, www.ntsb.gov/info/ATC_%20 Report_AA77.pdf.

"Statement by the President in His Address to the Nation," www.white house.gov/news/releases/2001/09/20010911-16.html.

Linda D. Kozaryn, "Sheila Moody's Story," American Forces Press Service, September 9, 2002, www.defenselink.mil/news/newsarticle.aspx?id =43484.

Christopher Braman and Sheila Moody, interviews with the authors.

Mark Buchanan, *Your God Is Too Safe* (Sisters, OR: Multnomah, 2001), 30.

Chapter 5: Hostage in Paradise

Photo: Bruce Olson during his early years with the Motilone Indians in the jungles of Colombia.

Story adapted from Bruce Olson with James Lund, *Bruchko and the Motilone Miracle* (Lake Mary, FL: Charisma, 2006). Used with permission. Also adapted in part from Susan DeVore Williams, *Charisma,* "Bruce Olson's Nine-Month Colombian Captivity," November 1989. Used with permission.

Mark Buchanan, *Your God Is Too Safe* (Sisters, OR: Multnomah, 2001), 14–15.

Chapter 6: The Last Lagoon

Photo: Ted Roberts examining the propeller of the Rio de Janeiro Maru in Chuuk Lagoon.

A shorter version of this story originally appeared in Ted Roberts and Pam Vredevelt, *Going Deeper* (Los Angeles: Foursquare Media, 2006).

Robert Kurson, *Shadow Divers* (New York: Random House, 2004).

Odyssey Adventures, www.trukodyssey.com.

Robert D. Ballard with Michael Hamilton Morgan, *Graveyards of the Pacific* (Washington DC: National Geographic Society, 2001).

Ted Roberts, interviews with the authors.

Chapter 7: Love and Loss in Iraq

Photo: Carrie and David McDonnall attracting a crowd of children in a marketplace in Sudan.

Adapted from Carrie McDonnall with Kristin Billerbeck, *Facing Terror* (Brentwood, TN: Integrity, 2005). Used with permission.

Carrie McDonnall, interviews with the authors.

Chapter 8: A Good Day to Die

Photo: Matt Moseley dangles from the Bell Long Ranger piloted by Boyd Clines during their rescue of Ivers Sims over the burning Fulton Bag and Cotton Mill.

Mike Santangelo, Mara Bovsun, and Allan Zullo, "At Rope's End," *The Greatest Firefighting Stories Never Told* (Kansas City: Andrews McMeel, 2002).

Boyd Clines, "Two Perfect Minutes," *Guideposts*, November 1999.

Jack Warner, "Hot Flames, Cool Heads," *Atlanta Journal-Constitution*, April 18, 1999.

Matt Moseley and Boyd Clines, interviews with the authors.

Chapter 9: I Want to Live

Photo: Brian Shul with "The Lady in Black," otherwise known as the SR-71 Blackbird spy plane.

Brian Shul, *Sled Driver* (Marysville, CA: Gallery One, 2003).

Brian Shul, "Danger Zone," *New Man*, November/December 2004.

Brian Shul, interviews with the authors.

Chapter 10: Deeper into Mystery

Photo: An avalanche pours down a face to the left of Slipstream on Mount Snowdome in the Canadian Rockies. The photo is taken from Slipstream itself.